IDENTITY
THEFT

Satan's Greatest Crime Against Humanity

DUANE SHERIFF

Identity Theft:
Satan's Greatest Crime Against Humanity
ISBN 9781680312201
Copyright © 2017 A. Duane Sheriff
Ebook: 978-1-68031-272-0
LP: 978-1-68031-273-7
HC:978-1-68031-274-4
First Edition: July 2017 under ISBN 9780998480909
Published by Harrison House Publishers
P.O. Box 310
Shippensburg, Pennsylvania 17257-0310
www.harrisonhouse.com

One thing I've learned in writing this book is that there's no such thing as "my book." Although I've handwritten every word of this book (several times actually), it has taken a team to build a ministry, and it is a team that has been responsible for bringing this book to publication.
Thank you to each and every team member who has played a part over the many years to see this become
"our book."

ENDORSEMENTS

No matter what you look like physically or who your parents are, you are not what God intended you to be. *Identity Theft* is a systematic, biblical, exegetical, and theological approach to origins, identity, purpose, morality, and destiny that offers spiritual transformation to the reader's life.

Dr. Dennis Lindsay
President and CEO of Christ for the Nations, Inc.

Even though this is Pastor Duane's first book, it's not his first rodeo! Taste and see for yourself how good this seasoned message really is, that has been penned from years of seasoned leadership. I know there will be many more books to follow, and I personally can't wait to see the impact upon this generation and the resulting legacy. What an honor it is to wholeheartedly recommend this book to you.

Daniel Amstutz
Dean of Worship & Arts, Director of Healing School
Charis Bible College

Identity Theft is a frank look at who we were, what we have become through the fall, and what we can become through the new birth and a new position in Christ. Duane uses his own personal examples to help make the meaning understood. You are about to be blessed and changed as you read.

Bob Yandian
Teaching Pastor

This is the most comprehensive book on identity I have read in over forty years of ministry. I would recommend it to every church and pastor as part of the curriculum of their discipleship program. The truths in this book will stabilize struggling Christians, energize growing Christians, and equip emerging leaders with tools to disciple others.

Greg Mohr
Speaker, Author, and Director of
Charis Bible College Colorado

CONTENTS

FOREWORD

By Andrew Wommack

President, Founder, and Chairman of Andrew Wommack Ministries

I believe Duane Sheriff is one of the leading ministers in the body of Christ today. His simple and yet profound revelation of God's Word is changing lives all over the world. And when combined with his humor, it's a recipe that makes God's Word so attractive that it's hard to resist. He is always one of the favorite teachers at our Charis Bible College.

Duane's revelation of the believer's true identity in Christ has to be one of the clearest presentations of these truths that I've ever heard. Truly, Satan has stolen the identity of the vast majority of believers. They don't know who they are, and thus, they don't know what they have and what they can do. This book will open your eyes to see yourself in Christ as never before.

I was saved at a young age and have been seeking God my whole life, but it wasn't until I saw who I was in Christ that my life really changed. In our spirits, we are already perfect, and the more we realize and understand that the more our outer lives will change as a result. The apostle Paul said in Philemon 1:6 that our faith becomes effective by acknowledging the good things that are in us in Christ Jesus.

In this book, Duane takes you through many scriptures that will open your eyes to a whole new you. You will find your true identity and come to understand how a holy God can love someone like you: It's because you are holy too. In your spirit, you are identical to Jesus. You don't have to wait until heaven to be changed.

One-third of your salvation is complete. Your spirit is as complete and perfect as it will ever be, and it's through that spirit that you can approach God and truly have a relationship with Him. This changes everything.

I'm excited you have chosen to read Duane's book. It's going to blow away mountains of unbelief and condemnation. You will rejoice like never before to know how much your Father in heaven loves you. If you will open up your heart and let the Holy Spirit enlighten you, you will never be the same.

Get ready! This is a life changer!

FOREWORD

By Jack Taylor
President of Dimensions Ministries, Melbourne, Florida

Duane Sheriff might well be one of God's best-kept secrets. The Scripture declares, "For nothing is concealed except to be revealed, and nothing hidden except to come to light" (Mark 4:22 HCSB)! I am highly suspicious that because of this volume, both Sheriff and the monumental work that God has done through him already will no longer be secret. Few men that I have ever known have labored so quietly, influenced more widely, and given more freely than this man. He deserves to be heard, and through this splendid treatise on an extremely vital subject, he will be.

Nothing in this wide world has so limited the church's influence, blunted the believer's effectiveness, or stolen from Christianity in general more than the theft of their most necessary component: an authentic identity as to their person and purpose. Mankind on earth will never rise above the level of the perception of who we are and why we are here. There has never been a theft so large and costly as that of essential identity. We have, both corporately and individually, been victims of a massive identity theft the world over. The only

3

strategic and lasting answer to this complex problem is the discovery of who and what God is and how this defines our own identity as His chosen ones to rule with Him in life here and in eternity hereafter.

This book identifies the burglar, the burgled, and the extent of the burglary, and it contains instructions for winning back the stolen goods that have long been held in the enemy's camp.

For those who read and heed the principles in this book, so skillfully articulated, precisely presented, and so powerfully illustrated and demonstrated, there will be the joys of experiencing the recovery of this stolen component so necessary to normal Christian living and successful Christian service in the body of Christ.

This powerful work will mean, for persons who accept and apply the principles presented here, a new and better life personally and a wider, more powerful ministry in general. Single chapters will change your life, thrill your heart, and revise your future.

I do not know of a book on this subject that is more profound, more effectively sequential, or more strikingly thorough than Identity Theft. It is an easy and pleasant read, well-illustrated, softly confronting, and frequently humorous. It efficiently mirrors the pleasant persona of one of the most unique communicators on the planet.

From one country boy to another, I say, "You done good, Buddy, really good!"

CHAPTER ONE
SWAMPY GROUND

As a kid, I was a swampy breeding ground for every lie and distortion the devil could sow into me. He sold me on lies about my value and worth and fed me distortions about my personhood and purpose in life. I was controlled and dominated by insecurities, complexes, and inferiorities. He planted the negatives, and I helped them all grow. My identity was summed up in one word: REJECT. It was as if the word was stamped on my forehead.

I struggled with my grades due to what is now known as dyslexia, which made reading difficult, and my spelling was atrocious (That's a huge word for me. Thank you, spellcheck.). Every day I struggled with thoughts of not being very smart and even that was being kind. A more honest version of things would be to consider myself dumb or stupid. I didn't excel in the usual school sports either because I was small and very thin in stature. On top of that, my looks weren't exactly up to par with the movie stars. My hair was curly and kinky and didn't seem normal on a "white boy." When I tried to grow it long in high school, it grew "up and out" instead, becoming a huge afro that nearly went from one shoulder to the other. The combination of my physical attributes was so bizarre that all my classmates called me "Q-tip."

As the years went by, things got worse; I succeeded at nothing I tried. Although I gave my life to Christ when I was nine years old, an overwhelming sense of deficiency dominated my thoughts and everything I did. You would expect that having a strong experience with God would fortify me, but it was overshadowed by the fact that no one in my family cared much about taking me to church. In fact, they didn't care much about going to church at all. After being saved, I began seeking God the best way I knew how. I recall a time in my early teens when I was trying to communicate my hunger for God. I told my dad I wanted to go to church every day, and his response was, "Son, that's not normal." He thought I needed some type of professional help. I was hungry for God but had no one to teach and train me, which is huge in our success as believers.

The church, which I thought would help me, was no help at all—constantly preaching about hell and damnation. Although they did teach that you become "a new creation" when you are born again, there was no evidence I was new. I wondered what was wrong. Maybe being "born again" wasn't all it was cracked up to be. No one explained to me how I could be born again and a new creation and still be such a mess. And no one in the church seemed to be living in any kind of victory over sin or everyday troubles.

The church only seemed to encourage my poor self-image because they considered that having a low opinion of yourself was a form of humility. I tried desperately to serve God, but I failed miserably at every turn. No matter how many times I committed to becoming more Christlike, I wasn't. By my senior year of high school, I gave up trying to serve God altogether. Feeling like a disappointment to everyone, including God, I jumped into the fast lane of self-destruction. I thought I deserved it and wasn't worthy of any of God's love or blessings.

Then, a crazy thing happened. I discovered that I was good at tennis. In fact, I was a "natural." One afternoon, I'd been hitting a ball against a brick wall at school when another kid standing nearby called out to me and said, "Hey, you're good, you ought to go out for the team." I kept hitting the ball, enjoying each time I felt that clean "thwack" as the ball connected with the racquet. I was hooked. I joined the team and began winning some local tennis tournaments. From there, I poured myself into it every day of every week, practicing long, arduous hours, hitting thousands and thousands of tennis balls. I studied the game to the point of mental strain because I was determined to absolutely perfect my stroke. I didn't make my bed or comb my hair; I just practiced. I was committed beyond reason, but it was such a great feeling to finally be good at something. I became obsessed. I lived like the world and played tennis like a maniac. I looked good when I played it, but on the inside, I was still a swampy breeding ground for the devil's lies.

There were many things that contributed to my "demise" and what I later understood to be an identity crisis. One of those contributing factors was my family and the environment in which I was raised. I love my family and I am not putting them down, but being a "Sheriff" meant I was always going to live the "low life." For generations, the Sheriffs identified themselves as poor and at the shallow end of the gene pool of humanity. They were so used to being defeated that it became comfortable, like a set of old, baggy clothes. They didn't realize there was something wrong with just expecting to survive, at best. In some ways, they even managed to become proud of it. They had plenty of excuses for being defeated, and it was clear that nobody should wreck those excuses by suddenly breaking free. If one of the members became prosperous, it would make the rest of the family look bad. If we all stayed poor, we could stick together. It seemed right to the family; they found security in sameness. Over time, it began to feel good being "nobody." The Sheriffs would say, "We aren't high-minded rich folk; we're regular folk."

This genetic and environmental identity was imposed on me as a child, so I used to think: I guess that's who we Sheriffs are. We're just poor folk, losers in life's lottery. That's just the way it is. Nevertheless, despite my family's attitude, and because of tennis, I managed to get into college. I was the first person on any branch of the family tree to accomplish that. You'd think everybody would celebrate it. You would expect them to say, "Wow! You're going to college! That's fantastic!" But no. My family said, "Who do you think you are? You just think you're better than the rest of us. Don't you know who you are, boy? Haven't you found your place, boy? Don't you know who we are?"

Before I go further, I want to note that the apostle Paul quoted the law with a tremendous blessing attached, saying, "'Honor your father and mother,' which is the first commandment with promise: 'that it may be well with you and you may live long on the earth'" (Ephesians 6:2-3). I want to live long on the earth, and I want things to go well with me. So it's difficult to mention things about my growing-up years or my family. There are no perfect families, and we all make mistakes in raising our children. I believe my parents did the best they could for us and loved us. I don't ever want to dishonor my parents, so I say the following with reverential fear and a desire to help others.

My family gave me a lousy identity. There was no ill will or harmful intent; they simply knew no better. They got it from the generations before them and passed it on to me. Not only that, but the perspective they held about life in general was godless. Even after I returned to God and began to preach, my own mother would never listen to me. She died never having heard me preach. I'm grateful she came to the Lord later in life and apologized to me on her deathbed. My younger brother had been killed in an automobile accident, and the stress and trauma of his death eventually led to the divorce of my parents and the unraveling of our family. My mother believed the lie that God was to blame. With bitterness in her heart, she resented God, church, and anyone, including me, for believing in and teaching about Him. My mother's message to me all along was: "You and what you do are not important."

At first, college gave me some confidence. They told me they had all the answers to my problems. They said all I needed was to develop a positive self-image and a high self-esteem. On the surface, that sounded good, but it ended up as a confusing concept. I struggled with reconciling the world's answers in comparison to the call of Jesus that says, "If anyone desires to come after Me, let him deny himself, and take up his cross, and follow Me" (Matthew 16:24).

I knew that scripture meant we were to be dependent on God. We're not supposed to be focused on ourselves or be selfish, and we're not supposed to live in pride or arrogance—acting as if we don't need God. The world, however, was all about "self" and "you can do it" and "you're good enough just as you are." I couldn't figure it out. I wanted to be good enough as I was, but deep down, I knew I wasn't. I had spent my whole life constantly dissatisfied with myself, so who else could find a good thing in me? It was obvious to everyone that I was completely insecure. I walked around in a cloud of inferiority complexes, frustrated to the nth degree. I couldn't get myself out of it. So, even though I was born again, I was as lost as a goose on a busy freeway. I was saved but living a totally defeated life. Seemingly, I had no power to change. What a crummy life!

All I had was tennis—my escape. Tennis gave me some sense of value, worth, and purpose for my life—some sense of a better identity. But I was running from God and covering up all my hurts and problems. I was hiding from myself, and I clung desperately to the game as if it were my salvation. I was going to turn pro and win Wimbledon and a million bucks. That was going to be my value. Then, one day in 1980 during my junior year of college, I met a certain girl and had an astounding vision.

2/5/20

CHAPTER TWO
THE VISION

My future life began with that girl named Sue. She believed that God's love would cure what ailed me, and she figured she was the right person for the job. She was living in an apartment just above the tennis courts where I'd been practicing and teaching tennis. At first, our paths only crossed occasionally, without much conversation ever taking place. Eventually, the opportunity presented itself, and I asked her if she'd like to play tennis sometime. Not being very athletic, she said, "I don't play tennis." In retrospect, I have to say she was not athletic **at all.** I won't say how I replied at the time...what I said wasn't very polite or appropriate. My speech was seasoned with something other than salt and grace. Still, she agreed to play, knowing that it was a door opening for her to share God's love with me.

After about thirty minutes of her not being able to hit the ball back to me—as in, not even once—I decided she was more than right. She absolutely could not play tennis! By this time, I was totally exhausted chasing the few balls she did hit—over the fence, into the parking lot, and off the porches that surrounded the courts. I was so winded and parched that I had to find a drink of water. We went up to her apartment for that drink, and that's when I discovered she lived in a completely different world than I did. There were Bibles and religious magazines all over the place. My first thought was, What have I gotten myself into? I could quickly see that Sue was a good Christian girl, which made me kind of jumpy. I was sure that my backslidden, running-from-God self was not going to help her stay that way, so I decided, I'm out of here! I asked where her restroom was so I could gather my thoughts and figure out how to politely dismiss myself so as not to offend her. But when I went in, I couldn't believe what I saw. There was a Bible on the back of the toilet. **A BIBLE ON THE TOILET!** I thought, Who puts a Bible on the back of the toilet?! I panicked, thinking, I've never met anyone this committed to Jesus! I only wanted to go to the bathroom, but instead, I encountered a seat in the Holy Vatican.

On my way back to the living room, Sue could tell I was nervous, so she gently offered me my glass of water. By then, I was desperate for it. Truthfully, I would have liked something a bit stronger, but I knew it was unlikely that any of that sort of stuff would be in her cabinet. Being all agitated, I asked her if it would be all right for me to run home (just a mile away), get a shower, change, and come back. She said that would be more than fine. What a relief! After I had got outside, I decided I was not going back there—ever.

I thought I was home-free. But my heart kept stirring me—there was something different about that girl. I thought she might know some things about God that I didn't. Deep down, I knew I still loved God, but I could not believe He still loved me. How could He, after I had so blatantly walked away from Him? Somehow, I got the idea that Sue might know something about that very thing, and what to do with the sins that weighed so heavily on me. I just had to find out the truth—good or bad. Had I gone too far to be retrieved?

In fact, the more I thought about it, I decided to prove to her that I was a lost cause, forever stuck in a negative world. So, I grabbed all the photo albums I had (this was pre-Facebook days) because I thought they were evidence of a man God could not love. I was going to show her every place I had been in my life, and that would surely seal the deal that I was beyond God's reach. The challenge was on. I fully expected her to agree that there was no hope—that I had gone way too far.

I charged back over there. When I arrived at her apartment, I wasted no time telling her all the horrible things I had done and what a miserable person I was. I just poured it all out, ready for rejection. Surely she could see the word REJECT on my forehead. But Sue didn't even flinch; she just looked at me with eyes of love and compassion. God seemed so real to her, so very close, as if He were right there in the room with her. How could this be? I began to ask questions. For hours, she patiently responded to all my doubts and all the ins and outs of my unbelief. I was moved beyond measure. It seemed amazing that she would sit there for such a long time as I droned on. Then again, the time of my transformation seemed short.

Within only those few hours, I was convinced of God's unconditional love, and I knew I had to decide. I struggled with it because I could see the goodness of God, but I still believed I was personally beyond repair. If there was an exception to what Sue was saying, I was it. I didn't think it was possible for God to forgive me because I had failed so badly. After all, I had known there was a call on my life when I was just a small child, but I had turned away. I had turned my back on God and started playing with fire in the devil's backyard.

From eight until midnight, I listened to Sue. Then I thought I had better let her get some sleep; she had to go to work in the morning. But as I stepped outside her door, a completely naked man came running down the breezeway, screaming and yelling at the top of his lungs. I thought, Man, it's midnight, and there's a crazy man on the loose! Sue had just told me about a guy who had been stalking her and slashed her tire just so he could knock on her door and "rescue" her. And now here a guy was buck naked! Even in my wretched condition, I had enough sense not to leave her alone in that situation. So, I went back into her apartment, and she took advantage of my chivalry by sharing the details of God's forgiveness for another four hours. As she ministered, I became convinced of God's immeasurable, incredible, unconditional love for me. By the time she finished, I was overcome with godly sorrow for the way I had been living, and I was ready to turn around.

The apostle Paul spoke of the goodness of God that leads men to repentance, and on that day with Sue, that goodness became a real experience in my life. It was so clear to me, and a feeling of deep refreshment came over me when I asked Him to help me receive the love and mercy He provided at the cross.

> *For [godly] sorrow that is in accord with the will of God produces a repentance without regret, leading to salvation; but worldly sorrow [the hopeless sorrow of those who do not believe] produces death.*
>
> 2 Corinthians 7:10 AMP

Unlike the world's sorrow, godly sorrow brings joy. It lifts a heavy burden and brings liberation. In the process of that sincere turning of my heart, I had a profound open vision of the crucifixion. My eyes were closed, but I saw everything as clear as day. I saw more than just a wooden cross or even Jesus on the cross; I saw the complete story of the gospel, like a drawing or a map that was laid out from the foundation of the world. I saw Jesus, but I also saw myself up there—in Him. I was inside of Jesus as if my body was fully stretched out as He was, like a hologram inside of Him. My full-grown body was within Him.

The gospel is all about the life, death, burial, resurrection, ascension, seating, and ruling and reigning of Jesus. And I saw all of that happening to me through Him. My sin was judged and punished in the flesh of Jesus when He bore my curse. I was within Him during His death, and I was transported within Him in His burial. Within Him I descended into the lower parts of the earth, but there I became blind. I was not actually blind, but I could not see anything. It was as if Jesus took His hand and moved it over my eyes, and we went "stealth." We became like a stealth plane—undetectable by radar. It seemed Jesus did not want me to experience hell at all. He protected me and shielded me from the horrors of it.

He spoiled principalities and powers and made a show of them openly, triumphing over them. I came up within Him and escaped from death. When He walked out of the tomb, I was within Him, walking out. When He was lifted up to heaven, I was lifted up within Him. And when He was seated at the right hand of the throne of God, I was seated within Him, ruling and reigning with Him in heavenly places.

My physical feet do tread this earth and my body is here, but my spirit man is in Jesus. The power that raised Him from the dead comes through me into my physical world. I can live a good life in the blessings of Abraham because I was crucified with Jesus and ultimately raised with Him to newness of life. The splendor of this shook me to the core of my being. For months, I couldn't even begin to contain or explain my gratitude for Him. When I would take communion at church, I would cry with tears of thanksgiving and joy; it seemed uncontrollable.

Waves of love washed over me and cleansed me day after day. I was on fire, but not consumed. I was aglow with light. I couldn't even sleep at night. I lost all my friends because I was crazy for Jesus, so Sue ended up being the only one I could talk to—the only friend I had. I would call her at two in the morning, asking, "Have you ever read this in the Bible?" "Have you ever heard about this?" "Did you know about that?" While I thought I was agitating and annoying her, she did not seem to mind. Then, since she was the only friend I had, I married her. (Although she was full of love and respect and kindness, I do have to admit that her being "smoking hot" certainly helped provoke the getting married part.) I've often reflected on what might have happened (or not happened) had it not been for that crazy streaker. I wish I could meet him and thank him for being so deranged; I came to see the heart of God because of it. God certainly used it for my good.

When I think about all those years I spent wondering why God felt so far away and all the hours I spent listening to preaching about weakness and sin, I think, Man, what a waste! Before this vision, I could never make sense of the gospel, because no matter how I sorted it, it always came to rules and regulations. Nobody seemed to be living in the power of it. They could barely even keep their own rules! But after I saw what happened on the cross, the gospel came into sharp focus. I saw the love of God and the tremendous gift of a new way to live. With that, I immediately lost all my passion for tennis, so I laid my racket down. Tennis had become an idol to me, and God had not been anywhere on the radar screen. Now, God was filling the screen, and tennis was nowhere in sight. I ended up losing my scholarship, but that was quite alright. All I wanted to do was God's plan.

I can't even describe who I was before that vision. I had deteriorated so much I'm ashamed to think about it. Most people wouldn't believe it anyway because God has changed me so much. I've been so transformed by the renewing of my mind that in Jesus I'm a whole different person than the Duane Sheriff the world knew before 1980.

The vision of the cross was a new start for me, and I was determined to understand the meaning of my vision in all its glory. I had to allow the Word of God and the Spirit of God to coach me. I was consumed by the Scriptures and found that I had a new and deep desire for revelation knowledge. How did what happened at the cross so intimately affect me? What did it do to my spirit?

I was like many other believers who don't know that their spirits were **radically changed at the new birth**—let alone how to walk in the newness of that life. How can anyone walk after the Spirit if they don't know who they are in the Spirit? How can anyone begin a transformation when they are totally dominated by their five physical senses rather than identifying with who they are in their spirit man? I knew I had more questions than answers, but I also knew that I had found the only source of genuine understanding: the cross and God's Word.

I don't believe everyone must have an open vision of the cross as I had. We are all different, and when we ask the Lord for help, He responds, knowing exactly what will touch our hearts. I do, however, believe we all need a clear revelation of what Jesus accomplished on the cross and the power of that work. I also believe my experience was not only for my sake but also for others in the body of Christ. I needed to understand God's grace so He could bring me back from being stuck in ruin. I needed the strength to endure the rejection and hardship that comes with sharing God's amazing grace in a very religious world where the traditions of men make the Word of God of no effect (Mark 7:13). Without that vision, I don't believe I would have the courage of my convictions that I have today.

I'm also certain that God will reveal Himself to you—just for you—in whatever way you need. If someone had shared God's love and forgiveness with me earlier in my life, the way Sue did in my twenties, I may not have needed a vision to reach me. I pray that God will use me in your life as He used Sue in mine—for your own discovery and full recovery.

And so began my journey from swampy ground to the promised land. It took some years of practice to get a grip on leaving my old life behind and embracing my new life in Christ—the amazing work of God in my life at the cross. During that time, I encountered another girl whose curious behavior got me thinking about the spirit world and the effects of the cross on my spirit man.

CHAPTER THREE

NOWHERE NEAR

t was in 1985, as I was still learning about who I was in Jesus, that I met a dear but somewhat spacey girl I will never forget. I flew out to California for a series of teachings in a church that I had never visited before, and afterward I thought, *This is the **last** time I'm going to California.* I was in rural, conservative California near the redwood forests, and since I'm a guy from the deep south, everything was strange to me. The gigantic trees only intensified the feeling that I was on another planet. I hadn't traveled very much, and I was still overcoming inferiority complexes and wrestling anxiety when it came to public speaking. I was also uneasy about my topic. I was bringing a message that I knew would rock the boat—a revolutionary picture of God's grace that many Christians found hard to accept. I was facing the possibility of hearing "Heresy! Heresy!" or worse, dead silence.

To top it off, I'm directionally challenged. Plain and simple, I get lost. I hate to admit it, but a friend of mine likes to say that I could fall off a building and get lost on the way down. This can be a problem because I also hate to be late; I think it's rude. But I was lost in California and panicking. I was going to be late for church, and I was the guest speaker!

So, even though men in general hate to ask for directions, I humbled myself and went into a small mom-and-pop grocery store. There was a young girl behind the counter. Bless her heart, I've named her Callie in my memories. She was a sweet girl, but she seemed to have lost multiple brain cells through whatever lifestyle choices she had made. Her body was there, but I don't know where she was. The conversation went like this:

"Ma'am, I'm lost, and I need help."

"You're not from around here, are you?"

"No ma'am. I'm looking for (such and such) church. Do you know where it is?"

"Uhhh...ye...yeah, yeah. I know where that is. Yeah.... I know where that is at, and yeah, yeah, uh-huh, yeah."

"Can you give me directions?"

"Uh...yeah. Yeah, I think I can get you there."

I waited while this girl tried to find some synapses that were actually firing. Have you ever been talking to somebody and been able to tell they were not really with you? That's how I felt with Callie. The whole time I was talking to her, she had that "deer in the headlights" look. She was just scratchin' and scratchin' for an answer. All at once, tiny firecrackers went off inside her head, sending little bits of light through her eyes. She got a revelation! She lit up! I lit up, because, yes, here it comes! The way out of here! We were standing face to face, and I was so eager to get going that I was hanging on her every word. And she said, "Uh...uh..." and my ears were all primed to hear.

"Do you know where the Walmart is?"

YES! Everybody knows where the Walmart is! That is the first thing you find in any town you go to. So yeah, I knew where the Walmart was. I was so excited. I was going to get what I needed. Then that girl looked me right in the eye and said,

"Well, it is nowhere near there."

At that point, she drifted off to some other place in her head, looking at candy bars on the shelf and bottles of water in the cooler. I stood there for a minute watching her, then decided to let her drift, and I went back out to the car. I could not wait to get on the phone and call my wife. I had to tell her, "The oddest thing just happened...."

To this day, neither Sue nor I can remember how I finally found the church, but I managed to get there. The meetings kicked up some dust and discussion. I got to know and enjoy those Californians, and I've been glad for any opportunity I've had to return. Yet, my most endearing memory is of Callie. She holds a special place in my heart, and I hope to get to meet her again one day. Callie had become something God never ordained her to be. She was as lost in life as I was in my directions. And years later, a basic but pivotal thought became crystal clear.

When I was in Callie's little mom-and-pop store, I didn't know where I was so I couldn't get to where I wanted to go. I needed a point of reference—a knowledge of where I was in relation to where I needed to be. Walmart was supposed to be my reference point to help me find my way to my destination—the church. That is a picture of man without God. When man is disconnected from God in this life, he is lost and doesn't know where he is. His reference point is in Adam— which means he is "away from God." His destination, however, is connected to God; his reference point being in Christ. The first step we must take to restore that fellowship with God through Christ is to recognize where we are—in Adam. Once that's recognized, we can plot a course from being in Adam to being in Christ.

Unlike Callie, God can show man where he is—lost, confused, in Adam, and fallen. Then by grace, He will direct us to where we need and were ordained to be before the beginning of the world—found in Christ.

I'm continually comparing Adam to Jesus. I think about what Satan did in Adam and how it affected all of mankind's identity. Then I think about what God did in Jesus, and how in a grand triumph, Jesus also affected mankind's identity once and for all. It's as stark as the difference between life and death. What Jesus did on the cross was a magnificent identity restoration. Jesus countered what Satan did in Adam in the garden—deceiving man and disconnecting us from our true reference point.

It was a colossal spiritual identity theft.

The whole premise of my message is summed up in a question and a statement:

"Do you know what Satan did to your identity in Adam?"

"Well, what God did for you in Christ is so huge, it's nowhere near there!"

The Message Bible expresses this very well:

> *Here it is in a nutshell: Just as one person [Adam] did it wrong and got us in all this trouble with sin and death, another person [Jesus] did it right and got us out of it. But more than just getting us out of trouble, he got us into life! One man said no to God and put many people in the wrong; one man said yes to God and put many in the right.*
>
> Romans 5:18-19 MSG [Brackets mine]

SATAN'S HIGH CRIME

According to the most recent statistic available from the U.S. Bureau of Justice, there were 17.6 million people in the United States alone who had their identities stolen in 2014, with financial losses racking up into the billions. That is huge, but when it happens to you personally, it's gargantuan. It paralyzes your entire life. If you lost your job during that crisis, you would have a hard time getting another one because in a credit check you would appear to be financially irresponsible. You would be held accountable for debt you did not authorize. It's an absolute character assassination. You could stand accused of terrible things you never participated in. Your purchasing power would plummet, and what used to be the ebb and flow of ordinary, daily living—buying food, gas, and clothes—would become a daunting task.

I have a friend who was a victim of identity theft and what that man went through was horrible. He said he wouldn't have wished it on his worst enemy. This is the perfect picture of Satan's high crime against humanity. It was a devastating spiritual identity theft. He's a smooth talker, that devil. While he was selling Adam a piece of oceanfront property in the Arabian desert, he swiped Adam's "kingdom-of-God ID card" right out of his wallet. He did this by getting Adam to doubt God's love, honesty, and generosity. Adam sinned and lost his sense of value and worth that had been given to him by his Creator. His source for all things pertaining to life and his identity were now placed in something besides God. Confusion, insecurity, and fear—all different forms of death—began to dominate him. Then Adam, as a father and a representative of man, passed that negative identity onto every man born after him.

In the Genesis account, when God showed up in the Garden of Eden to fellowship with Adam after he disobeyed, God asked him,

"Where are you?" Of course, God knew where he was, but evidently, Adam didn't have this information for himself. He was left with only a stark revelation: Because of what he had done, he was "not in Kansas anymore." That's right. Man was like Dorothy in *The Wizard of Oz* when a tornado plopped her house down in the middle of Munchkin Land.

Adam was transferred into another kingdom where he became lost, confused, and insecure. When God asked, "Where are you?" He was pointing out the change—the new condition Adam had brought upon himself. The Lord needed to show man where he was so He could lead him out. The first step to being saved is facing the harsh reality that you are indeed lost.

Adam said, "I was afraid because I was naked; and I hid myself." Then, God asked him, "Who told you that you were naked? Have you eaten of the tree of the knowledge of good and evil?" Notice again that God asked, "Who told you that you were naked?" God hadn't told him. Adam listened to somebody else and got information from an authority other than God. Unfortunately, the information redirected and redefined him. When Adam committed this treason, he lost his spiritual connection to God (a form of death). He lost his reference point, which was heavenly and God-focused, and he became earthly and man-focused. He became self-conscious instead of God-conscious. He lost the reality of his own value (in God). He no longer lived in the awareness of where he came from (God), who he belonged to (God), and what he could do (anything God told him to do).

Many people listen to what others say about them rather than what God says about them. Who told us we were ugly? Who told us we were fat? Who told us we were sorry, no good, worthless, or stupid? We all do a piece of stupid now and then, but we are not stupid.

Who's telling us all this stuff? Not God! Who says what's pretty anyway? Who decided that? *Cosmopolitan* and *Teen* magazines, Hollywood? All the media have cast their vote—television, shiny magazines, billboards, department stores, and more. We're bombarded with images everywhere we go. But taking our "what's cool" cues from the world is thinking with a horizontal reference point. It's asking man to determine what's beautiful, significant, or worthy about people. God never ordained for any of us to find our identity—our sense of value—in other people or from anything in the earth.

> *The lamp of the body is the eye. If therefore your eye is good [vertical, Christ centered], your whole body will be full of light. But if your eye is bad [horizontal, man centered], your whole body will be full of darkness. If therefore the light that is in you is darkness, how great is that darkness!*
>
> Matthew 6:22-23 [Brackets mine]

With Adam's help, Satan's crime was a catastrophe for us. It took nothing short of the Son of God Himself to come to earth to fix it. If you will listen to God—seeing Him as your reference point—I promise you will recover your identity. It is in God's Word that we discover who we are, what we have, and what we can do.

Our biggest problem in searching for answers to our many troubles is that we're looking in all the wrong places. Regardless of man's efforts to be in control, at the heart of it, he's usually looking for unshakeable love. Sadly, he usually goes to the wrong sources to find it. Through the philosophies of the so-called enlightened among us (politicians and professors of academia), recreational drug use (a.k.a. the drug culture), and the concept of "free love" (sexual promiscuity/perversion), we've become more confused and disoriented than ever. Then, when we have strife, division, and confusion, we think we can handle it. We think we can use our intelligence to work our way out of it or manage it or manipulate the circumstances in a way that will solve the problem. That's almost a joke! We need the Spirit and wisdom of God to be successful in our efforts.

> *Who is wise and understanding among you? Let him show by good conduct that his works are done in the meekness of wisdom. But if you have bitter envy and self-seeking in your hearts, do not boast and lie against the truth. This wisdom does not descend from above, but is earthly, sensual, demonic. For where envy and self-seeking exist, confusion and every evil thing are there. But the wisdom that is from above is first pure, then peaceable, gentle, willing to yield, full of mercy and good fruits, without partiality and without hypocrisy.*
>
> James 3:13-17

Two kinds of wisdom are revealed in this scripture. Wisdom of the earth is man's wisdom without God and is sensual—of the five senses—and demonic. There's no need for an explanation of this kind of wisdom. Then, there's the wisdom from above—God's wisdom—which is easily discerned because it's pure, peaceable, gentle, and true. God is the source of all true wisdom.

Most, if not all, of our social problems come from the identity crisis we have inherited from Adam. They are only conquered through the revelation of who we are as joint heirs with Jesus—sons and daughters of God, children of His wisdom and power.

> *His purpose was for the nations to seek after God and perhaps feel their way toward him and find him—though he is not far from any one of us. For in him we live and move*

and exist. As some of your own poets have said, "We are his offspring."

Acts 17:27-28 NLT

Paul said that God is not far from any man. He said when we receive Jesus, not only do we live and move and have our being in Him, but we are also the very offspring of God. It's in Jesus that we find life in abundance. It's in Jesus that we discover who we are and how we are to live in this world. Though we are certainly in this world, God has given us a command: Do not be of the world. We are not to be a part of its focus and value system because we are the offspring of God. We are to be of God's focus and value system. We are of His ability.

Jesus didn't die for us to just add some good stuff to our time on the earth. He didn't die just to improve us. No, Jesus brought a whole new kind of life, and He is the source of that life.

Jesus said to him, "I am **the way, the truth, and the life.** *No one comes to the Father except through Me.*

John 14:6 [Emphasis mine]

When Jesus said this, He wasn't just talking about going to heaven. That is indeed the connection to heaven, and there is no other access to the Father. There is no salvation outside of the cross. But Jesus came as a pattern Son to show us, out of the goodness and majesty of who He is, the way God intended for man to live. We are His sons and daughters, we bear His name, and we are His heirs in the earth. In a world full of lies and deception, false images and distortions, "Jesus is the Truth." He shows a new and living way to relate to God, to view our world, and to handle problems. "Jesus is the life"—a life in union with God bringing us a new quality and kind of existence, a life of abundance in God. He is the new source for our identity. He said, "I am The Way," and He is the absolute source for answers to life's difficult questions. He is our faithful, steadfast, and true reference point.

I heard a story that really helps illustrate the concept of Jesus being the way, the truth, and the life. In the early 1900s, a missionary in Africa had been working in a particular village and felt it was time to move on to the next village in the region. He diligently prepared for the day he was to leave and approached the leaders of the village to get directions to where he was to go. When he asked them for a map, all they did was refer him to a small man with a machete. Thinking that man would draw him a map or give him directions, the missionary asked him for a map to the next village. The man replied that he was the local map; he would show the missionary where to go by traveling with him.

The man was the "living map" of the local villages. As they journeyed together, the villager cut a path through the jungle with his machete and led the missionary on to the next village. The missionary was grateful to have been shown the way. He realized early in the journey that it was better to listen to the villager than to trust in his own directions. Had he strayed from the path being cut for him, he surely would have been lost in the jungle and perished on his own. In that jungle, the missionary found his way, his truth, and his life in that villager with a machete.

In the same way, as we navigate the jungle of life, we find our way, our truth, and our life in Jesus as He leads us, preserves us, and gives us true direction.

2/19/20

CHAPTER FOUR
ADAM VS. JESUS

God sees two groups of people in the world. This is not to say that He doesn't recognize different races, varieties of culture, or genders, but rather that God sees all of mankind in two heart conditions. People are either "in Adam" (the family of man) or "in Christ" (the family of God). In Adam all are separated from God here on earth first; if they stay in Adam, they are separated from God eternally. Those who are in Christ are reunited with God here on earth and eternally—just as if they never were apart from Him.

Most people don't like to think about death or eternity, and atheists like to put death in a neat little box by saying, "When it's over, it's over. That's all there is." But I'm telling you, everybody lives forever. Bodies die, but spirits don't. Spirits live forever with their identities. Real death—not just physical death but death of the spirit—is separation from God. It's the absence of everything good. It's the absence of light, joy, comfort, and peace. As descendants of Adam and because of the fall, all people are born into an identity connected with death. But the Holy Spirit continually draws each person toward the Father, which is an identity with life and abundance.

Simply put, there are two families in the world: Adam's family and God's family. You can choose to be a part of either one. Do you remember the old Addams Family television show? (The younger generation may have to Google it.) That was one messed-up family, but they thought everyone else was strange! Likewise, the real Adam's family—the family of the fallen world—is a wreck. They are spiritually blind, dysfunctional, and often lacking in common sense, but they look at Christians like we're the crazy ones. The truth is, we're not crazy but identified with Christ.

We're the real image of normal. Christians gathering with one another to provoke unto love and good works is normal. Being renewed in the spirit of our minds through the good Word of God is normal. Loving God, loving people, and serving both is normal. Healing is normal! Living lives that glorify God is normal! God is our Father:

> *Therefore be imitators of God [copy Him and follow His example], as well-beloved children [imitate their father].*
>
> Ephesians 5:1 AMP

There are enormous differences between Adam's family and God's family. Here are some examples:

WORLD VIEW (Adam's Family)	vs.	BIBLICAL VIEW (God's Family)
There is more than one way to God and many good gods to choose from.		There is one true God and one way to Him through Jesus Christ.

WORLD VIEW (Adam's Family)	vs.	BIBLICAL VIEW (God's Family)
The universe was created by a giant explosion that formed matter. This matter eventually became single-celled life forms that evolved into all of the vast creation we see today.		God created the universe and all things in it through the words of His mouth and separated man as a creature made in His image and likeness to take dominion and subdue the earth.
Morality is subjective and applicable as one sees fit. As time goes on, morality is always subject to change.		Morality is an absolute that never changes throughout time and should be continually taught to our children.
Abortion is a right for an individual woman because it is "her body," and she should be able to choose whatever she wants to fit her lifestyle.		Abortion is the shedding of an innocent, defenseless life. Our bodies and spirits belong to God.
Governments should be the caretakers of society, regardless of fiscal irresponsibility.		Governments are to be a terror to evil works and the sword of God upon evil that we might live quiet and peaceable lives. The church should be the one that feeds the hungry, clothes the naked, and visits those in prison.

As members of the family of God, we're continually called to check our thinking and adjust to God's opinion. His opinion is based on "in Christ" realities. His thoughts are to become our thoughts—in all aspects of life.

To point out one example in the different parameters of thought, Adam's family thinks in terms of justifying abortion: "It's not really a human being in the womb. It's just a mass of tissue." They come up with reasons abortion can be good, asking questions like, "What if the baby has Down Syndrome?" or "What if a baby will burden a single mother and consign her to poverty?" On the other hand, God's family thinks in terms of healing and restoration. We look for life-giving and life-honoring solutions. We believe in healing, and we believe God wills goodness in every area. We believe He will bring prosperity and blessing to our lives through faith in His goodness. No one is bound by disease or poverty when we have faith in God—faith in who He is and what He has already done for us.

Regarding abortion, we think in terms of blessing a childless couple through adoption. We believe in the value of every life, and we go toward it. We fight for life. This is a heart condition that comes from the life of God in us. Abortion is wrong on many levels and has lasting and painful consequences beyond our ability to comprehend. There's no amount of rhetoric or reasoning that can do away with that fact. I'm not in the business of condemning people for abortion or any other issue, weakness, or shortcoming. I only say this to provoke Christians to consider how they are thinking in general.

I want them to question themselves. "Am I thinking like God?" "Am I thinking from God's perspective?" "Am I thinking out of my new identity with Christ or out of my old, fallen identity in Adam?" "Is the mind of Christ dominating me, or is it the mind of Adam and those in Adam?" "Am I being spoiled through the philosophies of men in Adam?" (See Colossians 2:8.) I submit to you that many good

Christians have been clueless of the danger of thinking the way we thought when we were in Adam.

When we don't think as God thinks, our spirits are agitated. Without believing what God says about who we are, we're in a poor condition. We need to accept what God says about who we are and how He is at work on the inside of us.

> *For it is [not your strength, but it is] God who is effectively at work in you, both to will and to work [that is, strengthening, energizing, and creating in you the longing and the ability to fulfill your purpose] for His good pleasure.*
>
> Philippians 2:13 AMP

> *If then you were raised with Christ, seek those things which are above, where Christ is, sitting at the right hand of God. Set your mind on things above, not on things on the earth. For you died, and your life is hidden with Christ in God.*
>
> Colossians 3:1-3

And God has called us "more than conquerors."

> *Yet in all these things we are more than conquerors through Him who loved us.*
>
> Romans 8:37

Should we just live in our own opinion of our condition? Should we turn to others' opinions? Or should we accept God's opinion of our new condition in Christ? Is He or is He not at work within us? Is He or is He not the source of all that is good and powerful? Should we not press to live out what God declares about us?

DAVID vs. GOLIATH

The Scriptures make it clear that even though we were born as sinners, it was not because we committed sin in the womb or any personal sin thereafter.

> *For I was born a sinner—yes, from the moment my mother conceived me.*
>
> Psalm 51:5 NLT

King David wasn't saying that his mother committed adultery or fornication when she conceived him. He knew that he, like every man, had been born into sin through Adam's wrongdoing, which degraded the state of all mankind.

> *So then as through one trespass [Adam's sin] there resulted condemnation for **all** men, even so through one act of righteousness there resulted justification of life to all men. For just as through one man's disobedience [his failure to hear, his carelessness] the many were **made** sinners, so through the obedience of the one Man the many will be made righteous and acceptable to God and brought into right standing with Him.*
>
> Romans 5:18-19 AMP [Emphasis mine]

This means you had nothing to do with becoming a sinner. You received a spiritual handicap from your great-great-great-great, etc., grandfather Adam. All his descendants, including you, were born with that handicap. All of you came into this world in need of a helper or representative—someone who will stand in the gap for you. For instance, citizens of the United States are essentially handicapped because they cannot just go to Washington and have a talk with the president; they depend upon a representative. A representative stands on behalf of all the people in his or her district.

What a representative says and does profoundly affects every single person living in that area.

The Scriptures paint many pictures of God's love through "representative men," especially in the stories of the Old Testament. Yet of them all, none is clearer than the story of David and Goliath. Goliath was a huge man who stood nearly ten feet tall and carried weapons that weighed as much as the average man. Every day, he came out into the Valley of Elah near Judah, challenging the armies of Israel.

> *Goliath stood and shouted a taunt across to the Israelites. "Why are you all coming out to fight?" he called. "I am the Philistine champion, but you are only the servants of Saul. Choose **one man** to come down here and fight me! If he kills me, then we will be your slaves. But if I kill him, you will be our slaves! I defy the armies of Israel today! Send me a man who will fight me!"*
>
> 1 Samuel 17:8-10 NLT [Emphasis mine]

Goliath came out as a "representative man" on behalf of the Philistines. He hoped to provoke a "representative man" belonging to the armies of Israel to come out and fight him, but all the men of Israel were afraid. They thought Goliath was an insurmountable obstacle. However, the shepherd boy and future king of Israel named David knew better. He knew who he was in the eyes of God, and though he was just a boy, he accepted the challenge. He called on His Lord and dropped Goliath with a stone. He cut off Goliath's head with the man's own sword and held it up for all to see. At that moment, Israel was effectively "in David," because he had given them victory over the Philistines.

Then David ran over and pulled Goliath's sword from its sheath. David used it to kill him and cut off his head. When the Philistines saw that their champion was dead, they turned and ran. Then the men of Israel and Judah gave a great shout of triumph and rushed after the Philistines, chasing them as far as Gath and the gates of Ekron. The bodies of the dead and wounded Philistines were strewn all along the road from Shaaraim, as far as Gath and Ekron. Then the Israelite army returned and plundered the deserted Philistine camp.

1 Samuel 17:51-53 NLT

All of Israel rejoiced and divided the spoils. They themselves did not do anything to earn those spoils, but they received the reward **based on the accomplishment of their "representative man."** Because David overcame the enemy, Israel overcame. Because he achieved victory, they had victory. Jesus is our David who defeated the giant (Satan) and destroyed his armies (the powers of darkness). Jesus is the sole reason we have victory in this present life. And just as the armies of Israel rejoiced and praised David, we too will be giving our victorious Savior praise throughout the ages to come.

ADAM vs. JESUS

All of us could talk about a person who has impacted our personal lives—a teacher, a coach, a pastor, a relative—but no one has affected us more than Adam and Jesus. Adam represents decline, deformation, and condemnation. Jesus represents increase, clarity, goodness, rightness, and transformation.

In his letter to the Romans, the apostle Paul gives a description of the significance of these two representative men and the part each one has played in the life of mankind.

Wherefore, as by one man sin entered into the world, and death by sin; and so death passed upon all men, for that all have sinned: (For until the law sin was in the world: but sin is not imputed when there is no law. Nevertheless death reigned from Adam to Moses, even over them that had not sinned after the similitude of Adam's transgression, who is the figure of him that was to come. But not as the offence, so also is the free gift. For if through the offence of one [Adam] many be dead, much more the grace of God, and the gift by grace, which is by one man, Jesus Christ, hath abounded unto many. And not as it was by one that sinned [Adam], so is the gift: for the judgment was by one to condemnation, but the free gift is of many offences unto justification. For if by one man's offence death reigned by one [Adam]; much more they which receive abundance of grace and of the gift of righteousness shall reign in life by one, Jesus Christ. Therefore as by the offence of one judgment came upon all men to condemnation; even so by the righteousness of one [Jesus] the free gift came upon all men unto justification of life. For as by one man's disobedience [Adam] many were made sinners, so by the obedience of one [Jesus] shall many be made righteous.

Romans 5:12-19 KJV [Brackets mine]

Notice how a single man—Adam—got us all into sin and death. Later, another man—Jesus—got us out and into righteousness and life. Our first birth was in Adam, plunging us into death. Our second birth, our "new birth in Jesus," plunged us back into life. We were born into sin, and there is only one way out: being "born again." Essentially, all of Adam's descendants were cut off from the rightful inheritance that God had originally intended.

For example, suppose my great-great-grandfather had a close relationship with a powerful and wealthy man who decided to bequeath many treasures to Grandpa and all his descendants. Perpetual endowments were to be established for all of us. They would never run out. But then suppose my great-great-grandfather pulled a huge piece of stupid and betrayed the wealthy man through a foolish act, breaking his trust and permanently severing the relationship. As a result, my whole family became severed from the relationship, severed from the treasures that were intended for us. Because of my great-great-grandfather's actions, we were all suddenly cut off from the original will. Where Grandpa went, we went—even before we were born. What he got, we got, which was nothing! (Thanks a lot, Grandpa!)

IT AIN'T MY FAULT

We've all had the "it ain't my fault" syndrome at least once in our past. Yet when it comes to being a sinner, you really can say, "It ain't my fault." However, that is the extent of the finger pointing. It may not have been your fault you were born fallen, but it's your responsibility to cooperate with God's Word so you can recover from that state. Believers do not have the luxury of claiming "victim status." That's an attitude from Adam's family—not God.

Our society is collapsing because so many identify with "victim-ology." Pregnant? It's not your fault—society didn't provide enough protection or sex education for you. Can't keep a job? It's not your fault—you grew up in a dysfunctional family. Abuser? It's not your fault—your father was abusive. Burn yourself with hot coffee? It's not your fault—the restaurant didn't write "Really, really hot!" on the cup (Give me a break!). The world's excuses are limitless, and there seems to be an endless supply of lawyers eager to throw fuel on the fire for personal gain. But in Christ, we are called to rise above this cesspool. We are called to identify with a holy and powerful Father. And yes, I know, environmental circumstances can contribute to your troubles as well, but eventually, you have to take responsibility for your own actions, your own identity in life. It's a choice.

RELIGION vs. RELATIONSHIP

Religion and true Christianity are at odds with one another, and they are forever butting heads. The apostle James defines true religion as selflessness (James 1:26-27), which is in direct contrast to false religion that keeps man at the center of things. False religion persuades man to try to be and do good to earn favor and blessings with God. The true honoring of God is just believing that Jesus accomplished all we need at the cross. God did the work of retrieving man from the snare of the fowler by sending Jesus—a work that only can be received by faith so no flesh should glory in His presence. It is all His doing.

> *For by grace are ye saved through faith; and that not of yourselves: it is the gift of God: Not of works, lest any man should boast. For we are his workmanship, created in Christ Jesus unto good works, which God hath before ordained that we should walk in them.*
>
> Ephesians 2:8-10 KJV

Believing what God says about who we are is true faith. It also takes some courage because who God says we are in Jesus is pretty big! Religion gets it backward. Religion has us doing good works to achieve righteousness with God, to be or become good or holy. This is only the thinking of men—not God.

According to the Dictionary by Merriam-Webster, the definition of the word religion is an institutional system of beliefs held to with ardor (zeal). This definition implies, and the general public would agree, that religion has nothing to do with a living, breathing, personal relationship with a real God. Religion is merely a system of rules followed with a dedicated effort, many of which are nothing but the traditions of men that cancel out the effect of God's Word in our lives. People refer to Christianity, Buddhism, Hinduism, etc., as "religions," but true Christianity is not a religion at all. Christianity is a marriage relationship where a believer enters an intimate relationship with God. It's a wholehearted adoration of Him as a person. It's receiving His love and believing what He has said and done on our behalf (grace).

Religion incorrectly assumes that wrong-doing makes people sinners while right-doing makes them holy. Religion says when people sin, they're suddenly "out of fellowship" with God. Conversely, religion says doing "good" puts people back in fellowship with God. Whole groups of people think the things they do that are good will make them right in God's eyes—how they wear their hair or clothes, how they speak their prayers (lots of "thee" and "thou"), how much they give to the poor, how they are faithful to never miss church on a Sunday, or any number of things on their "do good" list. While Christians do much good, it's not our good-doing that makes us righteous before God. It's not our "good-doing" that gives us our identity. It is only Jesus. What He did covers all our shortcomings and every bit of our old "Adamness." All of our reliance is on the cross. All our effort to live a Christian life ought to come out of the knowledge that Christ in all His power lives within us. He is our savior; He is our focus.

Buddhists believe that wrongdoing in life could cause you to be reincarnated as a toad or a fly, whereas doing right might allow you to come back as a great and powerful person. The truth of the matter is that we don't get multiple shots at getting ourselves into a right state. There are no do-overs. We cannot climb the ladder of righteousness because no natural action can change the fact that we were fallen. A dog is a dog, a cow is a cow, and a man without Jesus is a man in a bad condition, a man in a deteriorating kingdom. Even given a thousand lifetimes, we could never bridge the gap that Adam created at the fall.

Think about it. Since it's not your personal sin that made you a sinner, your personal holiness cannot make you righteous. Jesus did this for us by becoming the bearer of all our sin. However, Jesus did not sin in order to be made sin; He just took ours. **Conversely, we don't need to do righteousness to be made righteous.** We just take His. Your family name of "Christian" says it all and does it all. It's all Jesus. We must let that truth grow in our hearts and bear fruit.

> *For He made Him who knew no sin to be sin for us, that we might become the righteousness of God in Him.*
>
> 2 Corinthians 5:21

If you can wrap your mind around the concept that Jesus, who knew no sin, was made sinful for us as a representative man, then it's easy to see how we can be made the righteousness of God. Though we have committed no true acts of righteousness, we receive the benefits of it. It was no harder on God to make us righteous with Jesus' righteousness than it was to make Jesus sin with our sin. Adam and Jesus were both men. One gave us an inheritance of death, while the other gave us an inheritance of life. Jesus gave us His life and power. We get to choose where we live as Christians—in Adam's mess or in Christ's victory and authority. And just in case this choice might seem a little too hard for some people, God gave us a clue:

> ...*I have set before you life and death, blessing and cursing; therefore* **choose life**, *that both you and your descendants may live.*
>
> Deuteronomy 30:19 [Emphasis mine]

CHAPTER FIVE
FLESH VS. SPIRIT

G od clearly tells us not to look at anyone according to the flesh. That is, we're not to make assessments of people only by what we see with our natural eyes or by emotions attached to old or prejudiced images.

> *And He died for all, that those who live should live no longer for themselves, but for Him who died for them and rose again. Therefore, from now on,* **we regard no one according to the flesh.** *Even though we have known Christ according to the flesh, yet now we know Him thus no longer.*
>
> 2 Corinthians 5:15-16 [Emphasis mine]

In the new birth, we make new attachments. There's a complete break from our previous perspectives, so we need to learn how to see everyone according to the spirit, including ourselves. I suspect that most people reading this have already made a commitment to Christ, but even so, a great many Christians still know people (and themselves) only in a physical, natural way.

Initially, the first generation of disciples only knew Jesus according to the flesh. For years, I thought that being with Jesus physically would have been such a blessing. I thought those disciples had it made! But I've matured some in the Lord and discovered that this is not true. In the Gospels, you can see that when the disciples looked at the Messiah in the natural, they often got it wrong. It would have been easy to think, *That can't be God. He's got a beard. His feet are dirty. He's hammering nails, and He just blew His nose!* Seeing Jesus in a physical way was actually a stumbling block. People said to one another, "Look, he's Mary's boy, and his brothers and sisters are right here with us." They wondered aloud, "Can anything good come out of Nazareth?" That is all identification after the flesh, and that is how we get it wrong in our own lives. We forget that because of the resurrection, the Spirit of God actually dwells **in us**—in our physical bodies. We are not just human.

When scripture says, "Know...no man after the flesh" (2 Corinthians 5:16 KJV), the first person you are not to know after the flesh is you. How are you supposed to accomplish that? You do it the same way you came to know Jesus—through the Word and the Spirit of God. None of us alive today have known Jesus after the flesh, yet if you're born again, you do indeed know Him. How? You found scriptures, and the Holy Spirit took the written Word and transitioned it into your heart to the living Word—Jesus. We know Him after the Word and Spirit.

Long ago, I decided to totally sell out to who God says I am, and because of that decision, I keep myself focused on what the Word says about me. I implore you to do the same. **You must quit seeing yourself as only a natural man or woman.** There's so much more to you than what you see in your bathroom mirror or your bank account or your job title. There's more to you than the shape of your body, your wit, or your skills at work. There's more to you than what any person has ever told you. When the Spirit of God dwells in your spirit, He reveals Jesus and the amazing effect of your restoration. As sons and daughters of God, we are—each of us—**in His likeness.**

For years, I've gone places and heard, "That's Duane Sheriff. Look at that hair. Did you catch that voice?" People would hear me ordering food and come around a corner looking for me; they just knew I was out there somewhere. They recognized something natural. They knew my high-pitched, squeaky voice. Even from a distance, they recognized my crazy, curly hair. When I look in the mirror in my bathroom, I see something I don't even want to describe—let's not go there! But when I look in the mirror of God's Word, the mirror of the spirit world, I see great things. I see the man God intended me to be in Christ. Because of my new condition in Jesus, I am righteous and holy, and a child of God. The more I walk in this newness of life, the more the things I say and do come into agreement with God. This is because all my **doing** comes out of my **being.** The deeds I do are simply a by-product of who I am.

Jesus declares, "You are the salt of the earth...you are the light of the world" (Matthew 5:13-14). Salt is potent; it can preserve, and it can destroy. It does these things by virtue of its nature. It does not strive to do these things. It has the effect of preserving and destroying simply because salt is salt, and things happen when it is applied. This is a point God makes about us as believers. Things happen in and around us because we are the salt of the earth, and we affect our surroundings for good.

Before refrigeration, meat was preserved with salt. Ancient armies often salted the earth of a conquered city, thereby ensuring there would be no resurrection of life among plants or animals. It left a lasting memory of total defeat and destruction. As salt, we can preserve people through our prayers, while at the same time destroying the works of Satan. We are also light. Light exposes and disposes of darkness. Light always overcomes darkness. As we learn to walk by faith in who we really are, we will increasingly expose the darkness of the world and break its power over people's lives.

Salt does what it does by nature. Believers do what they do by nature—our new righteous nature in Christ. This is a matter of heart-knowledge and not just head-knowledge. You don't have to attend Bible school or jump through theological hoops to receive revelation of the immense power that abides in you. To operate as salt and light, you must become more and more aware of who you are in Christ. Then, the things of the spirit will flow naturally. **This is a serious issue with God; it is not just frosting on the cake of salvation.** We are carrying God in the earth. We are His children with His attributes.

You are it! You are it **now,** so act like it.

If I insist on identifying myself only as a guy with long, nappy hair and a unique voice (flesh), I'm not being salt and light (spirit). I'm not obeying God.

> *For to be carnally minded is death, but to be spiritually minded is life and peace. Because the carnal mind is enmity against God; for it is not subject to the law of God, nor indeed can be. So then, those who are in the flesh cannot please God.*
>
> Romans 8:6-8

Because I know who I am, I go vertical to God. I am forever done with the horizontal! Zippo! Finito! I don't even ask my fellow man, "Do I look okay?" I've done all I can about that anyway; I comb my hair, I brush my teeth, and I look good—by faith! But in Jesus, I'm awesome, and so are you. In Jesus, you're so gorgeous, so anointed, and so beautiful. This body is just a rag in comparison. What you're looking at on the outside is a far cry from what you look like on the inside. All believers look better on the inside than they do on the outside. When I look at my brothers and sisters in Christ, I see them by the spirit—the potential, the power, and the purpose inside them are nothing less than incredible.

If I look at myself or someone else just as flesh and blood, we will both cry and get discouraged. It's imperative to understand that we've been imprinted with the wrong image by Satan and that we must now stop allowing what's around us to reinforce that fallen image. Has your family called you stupid or clumsy all your life? Did your schoolteachers say you were too loud or constantly a problem? Were you told you had ADHD? Did you hear, "You'll never amount to a hill of beans"? (I'm not sure what a hill of beans is, but I know it can't be good!)

Since I grew up with dyslexia, I always thought, I can never prosper because of this defect. That could not be further from the truth. I have overcome handicaps in more ways than one, and these days I only let dyslexia kick in whenever I hear the six o'clock news or some other outlet spouting off what is good and what isn't. What Satan did to man is so catastrophic that some form of "worldview dyslexia" would actually benefit a lot of people who believe all the lies being propagated by the media. The truth is usually the polar opposite of what the world says. We need to disengage from the identities the world pushes on us. We need to seriously engage with the better, robust identity that Jesus bought for us at the cross.

God's grace in conjunction with the new man inside can overcome anything we struggle with on the outside. Maybe your family has boxed you in psychologically with negative words. Maybe you were a bad kid growing up or you had a big ol' nose you hated or you flunked out of school or you struggled with depression. That's okay. You can't change your past behavior or your nose (at least not without surgery), but you can certainly change how you think. You can change your present and your future by continually looking unto Jesus, the author and finisher of your faith. God always causes you to triumph when you let what He says about you become the final authority. God's Word is not just ink and paper. It reveals the spirit world, and it highlights not only our spirit man in that world, but also our new identity. This new identity is in sharp contrast to the physical world.

> *It is the Spirit who gives life; the flesh profits nothing. The words that I speak to you are spirit, and they are life.*
>
> John 6:63

It is the spirit that profits us; the flesh profits little. You might be able to exercise and look young and attractive. You might be able to make lots of money, wear nice clothes, and drive a Corvette. But while those things are not wrong, they are not lasting. Those things won't fix the other problems in your life. The words that God has spoken to you are spirit and life. They will fix you on the inside and make everything on the outside come into a right standing with Him.

Living out of your spirit causes all other parts of your life to prosper and causes you to win every battle. It causes you to come into agreement with everything God says about you. The Word of God reveals what we look like in Christ—righteous and holy. What God says in His Word is exactly how and who you are in your born-again spirit. Because God's Word is spirit, it reveals spirit.

DIE TO YOUR OLD LIFE

Scripture repeatedly tells us, "The old has passed away." Consider the following translation to better understand what it means to have died to your old life:

*If it seems we are crazy, it is to bring glory to God. And if we are in our right minds, it is for your benefit. Either way, Christ's love controls us. Since we believe that Christ died for all, we also believe that **we have all died to our old life**. He died for everyone so that those who receive his new life will no longer live for themselves. Instead, they will live for Christ, who died and was raised for them. So we have stopped evaluating others from a human point of view. At one time we thought of Christ merely from a human point of view. How differently we know him now!*

2 Corinthians 5:13-16 NLT [Emphasis mine]

When Paul was on the road to Damascus, a light flashed down upon him, and in the brilliance, he heard God speak.

*As he journeyed he came near Damascus, and suddenly a light shone around him from heaven. Then he fell to the ground, and heard a voice saying to him, "Saul, Saul, why are you persecuting **Me**?"*

And he said, "Who are You, Lord?"

*Then the Lord said, **"I am Jesus, whom you are persecuting.** It is hard for you to kick against the goads."*

Acts 9:3-5 [Emphasis mine]

Instantly, Paul experienced a revelation of who Jesus is. He "woke up" to a new perception. He saw the new creation and how Jesus was united to His body (His people). Paul saw that to touch the church was to touch the eye of God. He knew that the Scriptures declared God's people to be the apple of His eye, one of the most sensitive parts of the body that needs to be protected and guarded. This is indisputable insight, establishing how important each individual person is to our Lord and how sensitive He is to even the smallest of our problems. Paul realized that he wasn't just persecuting the church; he was persecuting Jesus, who is one with His church. Believers are His body.

You and I are the body of Christ. What do you think being a part of the body of Christ looks like? Is that a body that identifies with weakness? If we are one with Christ, what should we look like? Paul saw this in a flash, and then he spent three and a half years in the Arabian desert renewing his mind to this "in Christ" reality. If Paul, a scholar, spent three and a half years renewing his mind to the reality of what the cross provided, what do you suppose we should do concerning this reality?

We need to wake up the same way Paul woke up. We are no longer deformed men and women without Christ. We are no longer identified with any of the destructive elements and warped perspectives of this world. The world can be loud and overbearing with its voice of despair, distrust, destructive desires of the flesh, and myriad forms of death. But we are commanded to listen to God. We are totally identified with Christ and His righteous condition and total victory over the world.

Living under the world's assessment, we become subtly oppressed by constant failure. There's always something better, bigger, shinier, prettier, stronger, and more desirable. Even if we manage to achieve the apex of success, we end up with emotional chaos because the things we thought we needed and wanted do not satisfy. Welcome to the collapse of marriages, the dissolving of close partnerships in business and friendships, and the splitting of churches. Living by what we see with our natural eyes delivers a boatload of misinterpretation, confusion, and insecurity in our daily interactions. We must learn to see ourselves, our spouses, our friends, and even our business associates through the eyes of God. If we commit to this perspective, we will begin to grow into the full stature of Christ and our relationships will prosper.

Here is another look at what happens in the new birth:

> *Because of this decision we don't evaluate people by what they have or how they look. We looked at the Messiah that way once and got it all wrong, as you know. We certainly don't look at him that way anymore. Now we look inside, and what we see is that anyone united with the Messiah gets a fresh start, is created new.* ***The old life is gone; a new life burgeons!***
>
> 2 Corinthians 5:16 MSG [Emphasis mine]

When we accept the work of the cross, we're so radically changed in our hearts that a new life burgeons. I absolutely love this word **burgeons.** It means to grow, develop, and expand rapidly. Some of its synonyms are flourish, thrive, escalate, boom, mushroom, and to rocket! Burgeoning is what we witness at springtime when things that look dead and depressing suddenly begin to come to life. Our job is now straightforward. We must be renewed to all that is brand-new in us. We are citizens of God's kingdom, but even more than that, we are children of the King Himself. We have new clothes—robes of righteousness. We have new weaponry—God's armor and the sword of the Spirit. We have a new perspective—whatever God wants is right and good, and we can do it. And we have a new focus—God and others.

HIS NAME IS JOHN

We must constantly practice living in the awareness of the Spirit. This is what allows us to dwell in peace in the midst of chaos so we may live daily in our true identity and purpose the way John the Baptist did. The life of John the Baptist was prophesied in the

Scriptures long before he was born. Contrary to Jewish tradition, he was not named Zacharias after his father. Rather, by a specific word from God to his parents, he was called *John*. John has a testimony that perfectly embodies how we are to identify ourselves as ambassadors of Christ in the earth. If we take a close look at his response to the Pharisees when they asked who he was, we obtain a key to understanding how to prove our new identity.

> *This was John's testimony when the Jewish leaders sent priests and Temple assistants from Jerusalem to ask John,* **"Who are you?"** *He came right out and said, "I am not the Messiah"* **"Well then, who are you?"** *they asked. "Are you Elijah?" "No," he replied.* **"Are you the Prophet we are expecting?"** *"No."* **"Then who are you?** *We need an answer for those who sent us. What do you have to say about yourself?" John replied in the words of the prophet Isaiah: "I am a voice shouting in the wilderness, 'Clear the way for the Lord's coming!'"*

John 1:19-23 NLT [Emphasis mine]

After being asked five various times who he was, John discovered his identity through the Scriptures that bore witness with the Spirit of God who was at work in Him. It would have been easy for him to lean on his father's esteemed position and say, "I'm the son of Zacharias, the priest," which was true after the flesh. Leaning on your family name or accomplishments is of flesh. He could have used his own miraculous birth by Elizabeth, who was barren, or even boasted he was first cousin to the Messiah, both of which were true. However, these things were true after the flesh, and so John gave his answer **according to the Scriptures.** Just as John discovered his identity in the Scriptures, we must discover our new identity there as well. That is where we find the declaration of our miraculous reconciliation to God and our new condition in Christ.

3|4|20

CHAPTER SIX

ORIGINAL PICTURES

Everything is identified by an original object or image. For instance, in a child's mind, the original image of a chair identifies that object forever. Early in life, the object was presented and someone in authority declared, "That's a chair." How does a child identify what has a wagging tail, four legs, and a bark? God did not shout from heaven, "Dog!" Early in the child's development, an actual dog or a picture was pointed to and called "dog." All the things a child learns to identify come from an original image coupled with a declaration from an authority in his life. That may sound ridiculously elementary, but I'm telling you, **as simple as that is, that's the simplicity of God's plan for man.**

God had an original picture of what man is supposed to be. Man was intended to have authority and work as a co-laborer with his Creator, taking the divine order of the garden out to the world. The original picture God painted of man in the garden was spectacular, but today's picture is nothing but a cheap counterfeit. Many people have never even considered there was an original picture, much less had a glimpse of it. Even though there's been blindness and confusion about this, I know I can't be the only one who looked at someone like Adolph Hitler and thought, *That's not even a human being. That's a monster!* I can't be the only one who looks at the masses today and thinks, *Something is not right here! What is wrong with this picture? This couldn't be the way God intended man to be.*

Even a lost man knows there's right from wrong. His God-given conscience bears witness to the truth. Unfortunately, man has become accustomed to identifying with a picture of sin, selfishness, weakness, and destruction. Man was originally crowned with glory and honor. Being created with glory means that he was something magnificent, beautiful, distinctive, and noble. He was something to take pleasure in and celebrate. The original creation was a special cause for love and respect. He was created good and kind. He was created for blessings and to be a blessing to others. He was created in vital union with God to perfectly reflect God's character, and the Father delighted to spend time with him.

Contrary to what the world thinks, man has not evolved; he has **devolved** into his current state. He didn't come from slime on the ocean and evolve to the mess we see (as the saying goes: from goo, to the zoo, to you). He came from God, crowned with the splendor and bliss of heaven but has since devolved to the slime we see today. Satan has blitzed and blighted the image of God in man to the point that it's totally unrecognizable. And I do mean *blitzed,* as in *blitzkrieg,* which is a powerful military maneuver executed against unsuspecting people. A blitzkrieg is designed to create sudden, overwhelming disorganization and confusion.

Satan's veiled actions were tantamount to a nuclear bomb exploding in Adam's heart, with the fallout swelling outward and corrupting everything beautiful around him. This evil victory was so pervasive that it has affected the entire universe—we're talking black holes and other dramas in our galaxy. But Jesus has put an end to all of that. He has come to reconcile all things back unto the Father. In the resurrection, He has reversed all the damage Adam created in the fall. We are the firstfruits of that reversal (1 Corinthians 15:16; James 1:18).

> *And so it is written, "The first man Adam became a living being." **The last Adam** became a life-giving spirit. However, the spiritual is not first, but the natural, and afterward the spiritual. The first man was of the earth, made of dust; **the second Man** is the Lord from heaven.*
>
> 1 Corinthians 15:45-47 [Emphasis mine]

Why is Jesus called the last Adam and the second man? Because Jesus is the picture that God originally intended for us through the first representative man, Adam. After Adam's transgression, Jesus came as the **second representative of man,** to restore that which was disfigured, making Him the **last Adam.** There won't ever be another because we won't ever need another. It's a done deal. All we have to do is submit to God and be conformed to His image by the renewing of our minds through His written Word.

Let's be honest. Most people in the church identify themselves with things in the earth—what they have, what they do, how they look. They see themselves through the paradigm of **how they feel** at any given moment, often affected and shaped by other people's opinions.

Many labor under an identity imposed by others or outward circumstances—skin color, a lack of education, living on the wrong side of the tracks, or not being one of the "beautiful people" (how sad). We're supposed to be like Jesus—not fallen Adam. Paul prayed:

> *That the God of our Lord Jesus Christ, the Father of glory, may give to you the spirit of wisdom and **revelation in the knowledge of Him**, the eyes of your understanding being*

enlightened; that you may know what is the hope of His calling, what are the riches of the glory of His inheritance in the saints.

Ephesians 1:17-18 [Emphasis mine]

This is the hope of His calling and a major part of our new inheritance as saints. Very few Christians have been actively taught to identify themselves this way: I am as Jesus is.

Love has been perfected among us in this: that we may have boldness in the day of judgment; because *as He is, so are we in this world.*

1 John 4:17 [Emphasis mine]

God is opening the eyes of our understanding to our new condition in Christ. In fact, we are the new creation—living in the riches of His glory we have inherited.

IDENTIFICATION: THE CLEAR DEFINITION

Identification means *to treat or consider as the same, to join or associate closely*, according to Collins English Dictionary. In other words, with whomever and whatever I'm identified, I'm closely associated or related to those parameters in thought, word, and deed. It means *sameness or oneness.*

Take a little test right now because it will help you understand my point. I will list a few names, and I want you to say the very first thought that comes to your mind. Ready?

Michael Jordan. Most likely, you immediately thought of basketball. Basketball formed and defined Michael Jordan's life; it became his identity. That man was born for basketball, and he became the best player that has ever graced this planet (That's not even debatable; it's a fact).

Next name: *Emmitt Smith.* Did you think of football? From a public perspective, football shaped Emmitt's personhood and individuality. You can't separate Emmitt Smith from football and the Dallas Cowboys.

It's the same thing when speaking of *Dr. Martin Luther King Jr.* The first thing that comes to mind is the Civil Rights Movement. The two are inseparably identified with each other.

How about the name *Mother Theresa?* Her name is synonymous with the demonstration of mercy and compassion to the sick and the poor.

What do you think when I mention *Ronald Reagan?* Some remember him as a movie star, although many of us think of politics and the Republican Party. Reagan had two strong identifications.

Finally, what about the name above every name? Jesus. Immediately, we think: *Savior, Son of God, the One who came and died for the sins of the world, Emmanuel God with us, the One who took our place, bore our punishment, and became sin with our sin.* When I hear the name of Jesus, I think of God's glory. I think of His true nature and personhood, which is liberal in goodness, overflowing with love, and lavish in giving. All these thoughts come back to the one central truth: Jesus identifies with us and our suffering that we may now identify with His victory. Jesus wholly identified with our fallen condition so we can wholly identify with Him in His shining, risen condition, ruling and reigning in this present life. The name of Jesus is synonymous with the new creation—our new condition and identity. You cannot separate Him from us or us from Him.

> *For he hath made him to be sin for us, who knew no sin;*
> *that we might be made the righteousness of God **in him**.*
>
> 2 Corinthians 5:21 KJV [Emphasis mine]

Jesus did everything right and nothing wrong. On the other hand, you and I have done nothing right in terms of salvation before accepting Christ. I'm not talking about physical accomplishments like winning a tennis match or getting an A on a math test. I mean we've never committed acts of righteousness that would earn the reward of being made the very righteousness of God.

Being made the righteousness of God means we are made equal with His character and virtue. We are made as the son or daughter of a king, with all the king's dominion assigned to us. The prophet Isaiah declared that our personal righteousness (righteous acts to gain anything from God) are as filthy rags. God alone did this thing for us; He alone gave us this right standing with Him through the work of Jesus on the cross. We have nothing to bring to the table but belief. Our part is simply to receive what Jesus did so we can be transformed by the quickening power of His life within us.

Just as Jesus was made sin without sinning, the will and power of God has made us righteous without works (personal holiness).

THREE PRIMARY IDENTIFICATIONS

There are three primary identifications that profoundly affect how we see ourselves:

- Short-term identification

- Long-term identification

- New, eternal identification

The first two are negative, generated from the world in which we live. They come from Adam. The third is our identification with Christ that reverses the negative effects of the first two.

Short-term identification is a direct connection with immediate family—father, mother, grandparents, etc. Many of our personal traits are inherited directly from our parents—bone structure, hair, eye color, skin pigment. We are white or black because our parents were white or black. We're short or tall because our lineage is predominantly short or tall. Most of who we are "after the flesh" is genetically passed down, and while some of these things can be changed simply enough, most either have to be accepted or overcome. We all have things about our flesh we don't like. If we have traits that cannot be changed, we must accept them and, perhaps, dress in a way that minimizes them. There are also things in our fallen nature that are negative habits passed down through family history, and we must consciously decide to conquer those.

Short-term identification is also impacted by environmental conditions. I was born into poverty, which shaped my psychological makeup. Poverty is more than just a physical condition of financial lack; it is a negative mindset. I thought poverty was part of who I was as a "Sheriff," and it took me years to break out of that perspective. Cultural stereotypes like "redneck," "hayseed," "Yankee," and any of hundreds of other derogatory labels will also impact us. Words spoken over us can lock us in an "attitude prison," which causes us to behave in certain ways and often seems impossible to escape. Fortunately, all things are possible to him who believes in God, and through our belief, we can break out.

Long-term identification is our connection to the rest of mankind. We are all part of the family of man, and we all inherited a condition of sin and death. The scripture says we have this treasure (Jesus) in earthen vessels or clay pots (our bodies) (see 2 Corinthians 4:7). Clay pots have cracks and leaks, so essentially, we are a bunch of crackpots! We're all flawed and fall short of the glory of God.

The first man came straight from God in the sense that he was a direct "hands-on" creation. God personally formed man from the dust of the ground, definitely showing the origin of all mankind— all from dirt. We can all trace our roots back to Adam, who was formed out of the ground. It doesn't matter what kind of dirt you are; without Christ, you are messed-up dirt. You are fallible in more ways than one and incapable of righteousness on your own. Just look at little kids; they will lie to their parents, cheat in a game, or sneak a cookie from the cookie jar without ever being taught to do so. That's because they have a fallen nature and are tempted by the enemy, Satan, who is continuously trying to lead them astray that he might destroy them. We all labor under this fact.

Years ago, a man named Alex Haley wrote a book called Roots, which was eventually produced as a television series. His intention was to help the black community in America. He wanted them to understand their heritage and family history—from atrocity to freedom—to build their esteem as a culture. Unfortunately, while Mr. Haley's work successfully showcases a culture valiantly overcoming a vicious evil, it had no long-term effect on the people he was trying to help. When he searched out the roots of the people, he didn't go back far enough. He stopped short of the true source, the first root in the downward spiral of man. Without identifying and fixing the problem at its root, there's no permanent change available. We need to go all the way back to Adam to understand this fallen, long-term identification.

The third identification—new and eternal—is by far the most profound. Its influence is overwhelmingly powerful and goes on forever. When you receive what Jesus purchased at the cross, you are grafted into the family tree of God, thereby obtaining an incorruptible inheritance that does not fade away. All the negative things you inherited from your immediate family or the family of man in Adam are overcome by the blood of the Lamb. No longer do you have to live under guilt, rejection, condemnation, and death. You now live unto God with authority over the destructive forces of the world. You have the spiritually genetic characteristics of Christ. This is spiritual DNA, your brand-new identity in Christ.

DNA is a mighty force. It always amazes me when I see people who look just like their mom or dad; the DNA traits are so strong they almost look cloned. Consider then, how our heavenly Father's spiritual DNA is stronger than any human DNA, and it is **in you**. It was put in when He took the stony heart out of your flesh and gave you a soft heart, a heart full of the Spirit of Christ. Once you are born again, you are recreated in your inner man—made into a **carbon copy of Jesus**.

By renewing your mind to this truth, the image of Jesus on the inside will begin to show up on the outside. You will become the head and not the tail, above and not beneath. You will be blessed coming in and blessed going out, a world overcomer, part of the holy nation of God, a king and a priest, a select soldier who is called to battle, and more than a conqueror through Him that loved us. How awesome is that?! That is more valuable than all the gold, silver, oil, and real estate in the world. Can you imagine being given a billion dollars and refusing to receive it? You know you would jump at it! How much more should you value this priceless inheritance from the one true God?

The revelation of my new spiritual position didn't come from my earthly father, James Silas Sheriff, or from the father of the human race, Adam. I got it from the Lord Jesus Christ Himself, who loved me and gave His life for me. When I saw this truth—ka-bam! I went from being a nobody in man's eyes to a special somebody in God's eyes. I went from being a reject to being accepted among the beloved. I went from a loser to a winner, from being overcome to overcoming, all because of my new identification. As I renew my mind to what the Word of God says about who I am, I progressively see and know myself as the glorious creation God intended for me. Who I am in Christ dominates my life. You cannot separate me from my identification with Jesus and His victory over sin, Satan, hell, death, and the grave any more than you could separate Martin Luther King from the Civil Rights Movement.

As a Christian, if you're not identifying with the new creation, you're not being your true self. The power of the Christian life will come to you as you grow in the knowledge of Jesus and the revelation of what He has accomplished in you.

Be dominated by your new identity; it trumps all negatives! In part, this is what it means to walk by faith and not by sight. The revelation of Christ's accomplishment on the cross and you being identified with Him will restore you to right perspectives and absolutely revolutionize your life.

3/11/20

CHAPTER SEVEN
MASTER COPY

From the very start, God created nothing but goodness for mankind. God's plan for man in Adam was that he be filled with glory and honor, beauty and dignity—literally covered by it. While Adam through sin lost all those good things, Jesus through His obedience recovered all that was lost.

Our new, redeemed identity is **Christ in us**, the hope of all glory. Once again we can be filled with beauty and dignity that brings praise to God. But the world does not have this heavenly perspective; it just keeps pushing against us, promoting corrupt ideas and decaying attitudes. We're surrounded by wrong thinking, peer pressure, money pressure, time pressure, and on and on it goes. Therefore, choices must be made.

Every hour of every day, you must decide: How will I see myself? Will I be in union with God through Christ and all of His provision for my life? Or will I be separated from God in Adam? Will I trust God?

From the beginning, there has always been a choice to make.

The Lord God made all sorts of trees grow up from the ground—trees that were beautiful and that produced delicious fruit. In the middle of the garden he placed the tree of life and the tree of the knowledge of good and evil.

Genesis 2:9 NLT

In this verse, we see a specific mention of two trees— the tree of life and also the tree of the knowledge of good and evil. The Amplified Bible, Classic Edition clarifies this further by specifying that the tree of knowledge represents **knowing the difference** between good and evil.

And out of the ground the Lord God made to grow every tree that is pleasant to the sight or to be desired—good (suitable, pleasant) for food; the tree of life also in the center of the garden, and the tree of the knowledge of [the difference between] good and evil and blessing and calamity.

Genesis 2:9 AMPC

A few verses later, we see that God put a demand on man:

And the Lord God commanded the man, saying, "You may freely eat of every tree of the garden; but of the tree of the knowledge of good and evil and blessing and calamity you shall not eat, for in the day that you eat of it eat you shall surely die.

Genesis 2:16-17 AMPC

THE TREE—THE CHOICE

People think this garden business was all about no—"No, don't eat of the tree of the knowledge of good and evil." "No, you can't have it because I am God, and I restrict you." The "no" part was important, but the bigger part was about yes. The garden as a whole was also about a great big *yes.* "Yes, please eat! Eat of every tree of the garden." There was only one single no among a thousand yeses. And those yeses included the tree of life. Some people think the story of the garden is just for little kids in their Sunday school classes—a print out for them to color leaves green and the apple red. But the creation of Adam and the events in the Garden of Eden are more than just a story. Adam and Eve in the garden represent a strong message. In them, we see God's original plan for man, which was **nothing but good.**

> *Every good thing given and every perfect gift is from above; it comes down from the Father of lights [the Creator and Sustainer of the heavens], in whom there is no variation [no rising or setting] or shadow cast by His turning [for He is perfect and never changes].*
>
> James 1:17 AMP

You need to understand at the most basic level that God's attributes are clearly defined—as plain as black and white. God is good, and the devil is bad. There's no question about it.

> *The thief* (Satan*) comes only in order to steal and kill and destroy. I* (Jesus) *came that they may have and enjoy life, and have it in abundance [to the full, till it overflows].*
>
> John 10:10 AMP [Parentheses mine]

All God requires from us is a choice—a choice to love Him back or a choice to reject Him. Will we choose to love Him back or doubt His love for us? The Tree of Knowledge of Good and Evil in the Garden of Eden represented that ability to choose. If Adam had chosen to love God back (by believing Him, by being obedient to Him), he would have come to a godly knowledge of good and evil. His view would have been through the lens of love and truth. God would have taught him good from evil from His own perspective, not from fallen man's concept that gets everything twisted up, clouded, and confused. A godly perspective of good and evil is an anchor in a turbulent world, helping us to reject the ways of the world and confidently embrace the blessings of God even in the face of impossible odds.

Armed with this truth, man can be a copy of the Master—he can think like his heavenly Father thinks, he can do as God does, and he can say what God says. Then, as the Scriptures teach, everything he puts his hand to will prosper.

Without God, our view of good and evil is ill-informed and generated and altered by the things of the world—by money, material possessions, and emotions and offenses. The world says that all Christians are narrow-minded and bigoted. The world says the government should tell us what is okay and not okay when it comes to our speech (political correctness). The world says euthanizing the elderly is a mercy. The world expects the worst of everything. It accepts disease as normal and divorce as probable and minor. It gives rewards for mothers who have children out of wedlock and then complain about the cost, both financially and socially. Whether you realize it or not, these attitudes are all part of an identification with fallen Adam.

> *What sorrow for those who say that evil is good and good is evil, that dark is light and light is dark, that bitter is sweet and sweet is bitter.*
>
> Isaiah 5:20 NLT

The world seems to think it knows better and says things like, "I went to college, and I have knowledge." "I know the difference between good and evil." "I have a Ph.D. in what the world says about things."

In my many years in ministry, I have been up close and personal with all the "progressive" ideas and purposes of Adam's family. God had a good, clear handle on the difference between good and evil, and He would have shared it with Adam. Instead, Adam was deceived into thinking there was something better than God's direction, and he ate of the tree that gave him a knowledge of good and evil through the lens of death and condemnation.

Let me explain this. Cancer is a despicable, horrible evil that strikes fear in the hearts of people throughout the world. It brings death and pain to millions. In spite of its horror, there are two distinct perspectives on it. A doctor sees the cancer from a distance; a doctor can have intimate knowledge of the disease while remaining in perfect health (life). Patients see cancer up close. They experience pain, fear, and a heavy cloud that can overshadow them with hopelessness (death). Both the doctor and the patient have intimate knowledge of the condition, yet they see it through radically different viewpoints. Like the doctor, God knows good and evil while being totally separated from evil, never touching or being touched by it. From His vantage point, He's able to properly and perfectly discern good from evil.

Man without God has a knowledge of good and evil through the haunting sense and lens of impending death. His separation from God causes his discernment of good and evil to be clouded at best. The instant he calls upon the name of the Lord, that paradigm is changed. With this "corrected vision," man can see that God's life is greater than death. Man is then separated from evil by the promise of God's redemption, the blood of Jesus.

The day Adam ate of the Tree of Knowledge of Good and Evil, God told him he would surely die. True, Adam lived over nine hundred years after this transgression, but that's because physical death and spiritual death are two very different things.

> *Therefore we are always confident, knowing that, while we are at home in the body, we are absent from the Lord: (For we walk by faith, not by sight:) We are confident, I say, and willing rather to be absent from the body, and to be present with the Lord.*
>
> 2 Corinthians 5:6-8 KJV

> *For as the body without the spirit is dead, so faith without works is dead also.*
>
> James 2:26 KJV

Physical death is explained in the Word as a person being separated from his body. The death that began the day Adam ate of the tree was an existence apart from God or spiritual death. That day, he was separated from God's life and light in his spirit man, leaving a vacuum for death and darkness to set in. This is what I call the "cycle of the living dead." This brought us our inheritance in Adam: depression, sickness, poverty, sin, confusion, insecurity— all manifestations of this death. Adam was physically alive, but his spiritual death dominated his thoughts and actions. Then, the ultimate effect of Adam's transgression took its toll in his physical body. The biblical record clearly shows that man's life span grew shorter and shorter after Adam and Eve sinned. This is an example of how man has **DE-volved**. It is an example of man living in a "non-Christ" identity.

When Adam and Eve rebelled against God and ate of the forbidden fruit, God literally ran them out of the garden. Many people think God was angry, kicking them out to punish them. But actually, God was protecting them. He did not want them to live eternally separated from Him. Had they stayed in the garden and eaten of the Tree of Life in that fallen state, they would have lived forever in a mortal, corruptible body subject to disease, pain, and suffering. That is far away from God's heart and His plan for mankind.

In the garden, war was declared. Satan challenged God by stealing His most precious creation, and God had to take immediate action in order to guarantee the reconciliation of all things back to Himself. He posted a guard at the gates to protect the way to the Tree of Life, and He immediately began to speak of a deliverer. Jesus— the second man and the last Adam—would come through the seed of woman and crush the head of the serpent. God has never been caught off guard. He knew what Adam would do, and He had a plan of redemption that would allow Adam and his descendants to once again choose life and once again be identified with Him.

BAD MASTER—BAD COPIES

For centuries, people have wondered which came first—the chicken or the egg. Well, I'll tell you, it's the chicken! In Genesis, we see that everything was created in maturity, bearing seed for the purpose of reproduction—man, animals, and plants. God commanded them to reproduce after their own kind. The answer to the question of which came first is that God did not speak to a tree seed but to a tree. He created everything in maturity, containing seed that would reproduce after its own kind. He created Adam as a full-grown man and not a baby. As the father of all his descendants, Adam was a master copy with perfect seed to create perfect duplicates.

Adam was to fill the earth with people made in God's image from the inside out, people whose identity was crowned with glory and honor. When Adam sinned, it affected the seed of man, meaning that while Adam reproduced after his own kind, it was the wrong kind. After Adam's seed became corrupted, every duplicate was corrupted. Every person born after Adam's sin was affected, and every seed was guaranteed to reproduce corruption after its own kind. The seed passes down through the father to the children through the blood. This is why Jesus could not have a natural father. Medically, when the sperm unites with the egg, the blood is formed. That is why the virgin birth is so important. It is not debatable. There had to be a virgin birth in order for us to be saved. The corrupted seed of man had to be bypassed in order to get another, unstained master copy into the earth. Jesus is the master copy who is filling the earth with duplicates after His kind, and so we're born again of an incorruptible seed.

Years ago, when Victory Life Church began, we started to make cassette tapes of all the messages and distribute them for free. We would make a master copy, put it on a duplicating machine, and create hundreds of thousands of duplicates. We're doing the same thing now on digital media by the millions. I do endeavor with all my heart to speak with accuracy, simplicity, clarity, and sanity, without stuttering or flubbing up the words. I try to choose my words carefully to avoid making grammatical or theological mistakes. Why? Because if I mess up, it gets on the master, and then every duplicate is messed up by the millions.

Originally, Adam was a good master copy with seed after his own kind. The point is, God had a charge for Adam: Stay connected to Me, love Me with all your heart, might, and soul, and fill the earth with people who are just like you. But Adam didn't do that. Because of his sin, he became a flawed master copy. All the "dupes" are messed up. And in case you're confused as to who the "dupes" are, it's you and me when we were in Adam.

So, God took measures into His own hands and created a new master copy by sending Jesus into the earth as a man—the second man, the perfect man, the last Adam. God bypassed the seed of man with the seed of woman (the virgin birth) to get a new, perfect master copy into the earth. Through this avenue, God was able to fulfill the original mandate and fill the earth with God's character traits and nature.

I'm here to tell you that Jesus didn't mess up the master copy. He obeyed God to the letter. He went to the cross bearing the weight of all our trespasses. He died a horrible death and was buried. But He rose up victorious and was seated in heavenly places. Now, His Spirit is filling our hearts and filling the earth with copies made after His image—made in the likeness of The Master. This is awesome! This is our ID card. We are no longer messed up "dupes" in Adam, but now we are new creations in Christ.

WHAT STATE ARE YOU IN?

When my wife Sue was pregnant with our daughter, Shekinah, we were praying about where we needed to live. At that time, I was helping another minister with his church. It was going well. The church was growing, but I had taken on that work for a season. It was for a good purpose, but I knew it was temporary (or so I thought). So, Sue and I had a lot of questions. Was it possible that we were to stay? Was it even God's will for us to continue pastoring? We knew that we would eventually be "planted" somewhere because that's God's will for all His people; we all need to put roots down at some point. I know there are traveling evangelists and missionaries, etc., but we put roots down in knowing God's direction for us and what we should work at building.

Sue and I just wanted to do the will of God, but at the time, I wasn't sure exactly what that was. We prayed specifically, even going so far as to ask God if we were to move to Texas, which had some opportunities. As I said, Sue was pregnant, and I'm sure you understand that wherever a pregnant woman goes, the baby also goes. Everything the pregnant woman does, the baby does. What the pregnant woman eats, the baby eats. There is *identification* between the mother and the child. Well, we got to thinking, *If we live in Oklahoma and Shekinah is born, she will be called an "Okie," and everything will be "OK"!*

Notice that what she would be called had nothing to do with her, but it had everything to do with the state that her mother lived in when she was born. If we had moved twenty miles south to the state of Texas and she was born there, she would have been called a Texan. The point is that none of us chose what state we were born in or what we **were** called, but now we can choose what state we reside in and what we **will** *be* called—the tasks for which our lives are designated. That is a picture of the new birth.

We were all in Adam like Shekinah was in Sue, born in a certain state. Had Adam remained in right relationship with God, we would have been born into the same state and called righteous and truly holy. But Adam moved from right with God to separate from God. We were in him, so when he moved, we moved, and then we were born in the state of sin and called sinners. But anyone can move to another state by being reborn. Lightning can strike your brain, wisdom and revelation can overtake you, and you can have an epiphany. You can cross the spiritual border into a state of life and peace, and from then on, you will be called a child of God, a saint.

In Adam's "state," our spiritual eyesight is darkened, and we are called sinners. In Jesus' "state," our spiritual eyes are opened, and we are called saints. Being a saint doesn't mean you are perfect; it means you put your faith in the goodness that has been purchased for you by the Perfect One—Jesus. It means you are **blameless**, because you have become just like Jesus in your inward man. He did it all for you at the cross.

In nearly every letter that Paul wrote to the churches, he referred to the people who gathered there as "saints" because he had had the revelation of righteousness by faith in Jesus. Some religious groups have decided that only the leadership can be designated as saints, but Paul specifically called the general body of believers saints. Becoming a saint—becoming an entirely different kind of person—is not just for a select few. Jesus bore sin for the whole world. He gave us the ability to move from one state to another. It's a choice. Choosing to remain in a fallen state has both temporal and eternal consequences. A life without God is a life without true, enduring love, and all the blessings and protection that love provides.

Even worse, leaving this earthly life in a state of death leads to what the Scriptures call the *second death,* an eternal existence apart from God. But again, I tell you that anyone can choose. You can be an Okie, or you can be a Texan. You can be a sinner, or you can be a saint. Even though none of us got to choose what state we were born in and what we were called, all of us get to choose which state we will reside in and what we will be called for eternity.

Choose an identity in Christ. Choose life! And take on the image of the Master.

3/18/20

CHAPTER EIGHT
NOT AS...SO IS...

know there are some brilliant, holy people who read the Bible and a light just instantly comes on in their heads. Angels sing, radiant beams shine down from heaven, and they experience great revelation. I wish I could just touch those people. I'm sure they must glow in the dark! As for me, when I read the Bible, sometimes my brain goes *Tilt—Tilt—Tilt!* I'll be reading along, getting real understanding, and then stumble across something that doesn't make a lick of sense to me. There are times what I'm reading seems to contradict other parts of the Bible, so of course I think, *This can't be right.* But over the years, I've learned to discard my carnal mind and utterly trust the Holy Spirit, the great Teacher, to reveal the hidden mysteries of the Scriptures.

> *The mind governed by the flesh is hostile to God; it does not submit to God's law, nor can it do so.*
>
> Romans 8:7 NIV

As I've submitted to God, He's been faithful. He's always illuminated the difficult passages as I continued to study them out. One scripture in particular vexed me for years:

> *But **not as** the offense, **so also is** the free gift. For if through the offense of one many be dead, much more the grace of God, and the gift by grace, which is by one man, Jesus Christ, hath abounded unto many. And **not as** it was by one that sinned, **so is** the gift: for the judgment was by one to condemnation, but the free gift is of many offenses unto justification*
>
> Romans 5:15-16 KJV [Emphasis mine]

COMPARISON BY CONTRAST

How could something be a "not as—so is"? That's not even good English! Far be it from me to judge what is good English. I can butcher the English language better than most, but even I know that "not as—so is" just ain't good English (at least not in my circle of friends and family). I've never heard anybody say "not as a piano so is a violin" or "not as Frosted Flakes so is Cocoa Puffs." But the Holy Spirit showed me that a "not as—so is" is a comparison by contrast. It compares two things that have basic similarities and yet are so radically different there's really no comparison between them at all. Here are a few examples:

Not as a fish bowl so is the Atlantic Ocean. Both have fish, both have water, both have weeds, yet there's virtually no comparison between the two.

Not as a candle so is the noonday sun. Both are on fire, both are hot, and both give light and expel darkness. But while their basic properties are the same, their functions are incomparable.

Not as a firecracker, so is an atomic bomb. Both of them explode, both make noise, and both have smoke. But there's no way to even begin to compare the power and effect of a firecracker with that of an atomic bomb.

That's what the apostle Paul was conveying to the Christian world. When Adam rebelled against God, he changed all of mankind. When Jesus suffered, died, and rose again, He also changed all of mankind. But the good that came through Jesus was incomparably greater than the damage that came through Adam. Not as the identity theft that Satan perpetrated in Adam so is the recovery of our true identity—to glorious proportions in Christ and brilliantly orchestrated by God at the cross.

Here are just a few similarities between the first Adam and the last Adam—Jesus:

- **Both men were similar in that they lived on the earth.**

- **Both men represented all of mankind.**

- **Both men were given extreme authority by God.**

- **Both men were tempted in a garden.** Adam failed in the Garden of Eden. Jesus triumphed over Satan in the Garden of Gethsemane.

- **Both men ate of a tree.** Adam ate of a tree of disobedience, plunging the world into darkness. Jesus ate of a tree of obedience—the cross—paying the full price to buy all of mankind back and return them to light.

- **Both were direct, hands-on creations of God.** Adam was born from the dust of the earth, and Jesus was formed in the womb of Mary. Both came directly from God.

While there are similarities between these two men, there is **no comparison** between what Adam did in the fall and what Jesus did in the resurrection.

OH DEATH, WHERE IS THY STING?

Death is very real. We all encounter it more often than we like, whether it's a family member, a friend, or a child we hear about on the news. The loss is painful, and it feels and appears to be final. But there's so much life that came from God through Jesus Christ that one day He will come back and literally swallow up all death in victory from the beginning of time unto the end.

> *"O Death, where is your sting? O Hades, where is your victory?" The sting of death is sin, and the strength of sin is the law. But thanks be to God, who gives us the victory through our Lord Jesus Christ. Therefore, my beloved brethren, be steadfast, immovable, always abounding in the work of the Lord, knowing that your labor is not in vain in the Lord.*
>
> 1 Corinthians 15:55-58

All of the hurt and pain will be wiped from our eyes, and there will be no memory of anguish, sorrow, or death. There's indeed a comparison between what the devil did in Adam to what God did in Christ. But during our lifetimes and even more so for all of eternity, it's like a teaspoon of water tipped onto the ground compared to a worldwide tsunami. There is no comparison at all. The only way to say it is this: "not as...so is...."

Not as the death that Adam's sin brought all man—**so is** the life that Jesus and His righteousness brought us all who believe.

Not as the effects of Adam's fall on us all—**so is** the result of Jesus' resurrection on us who believe forever.

Over the years, God has used different Bible translations to help me understand things that caused me to struggle. I've grown fond of the New Living Translation, and I enjoy the Amplified Bible, which I affectionately call the "Ladies' Bible" because it has about twice the number of words that other translations have. Since we all know that women, on average, speak about twice as many words as men, I figured God made a Bible just for them (of course, I'm just kidding!). The Amplified is very expressive, much like my wife. I like it because it elaborates on verses, helping to clarify what's otherwise hard to understand. The "King Jimmy" is awesome, but it has a tendency to be challenging on some verses.

The Amplified Bible, Classic Edition clarifies below:

> But God's free gift is not at all to be compared to the trespass [His grace is out of all proportion to the fall of man]. For if many died through one man's falling away (his lapse, his offense), much more profusely did God's grace and the free gift [that comes] through the undeserved favor of the one Man Jesus Christ abound and overflow to and for [the benefit of] many.
>
> Romans 5:15-16 AMPC

Think again about my friend Callie from California. She asked me if I knew where the Walmart was and then blurted out, "Well, it's nowhere near there!" In the same way, God is saying to you: The guilt and condemnation, the deterioration, and all the sin that came out of Adam's disobedience is nowhere near there. All the pain and bad junk you suffer in this natural life is nowhere near there. And the goodness I did for you in Christ is **nowhere near there!**

What God did in Christ is far superior and far supersedes anything Satan did in Adam.

The Message translation of the Bible illuminates this very well:

> *Even those who didn't sin precisely as Adam did by disobeying a specific command of God still had to experience this termination of life, this separation from God. But Adam, **who got us into this,** also points ahead to **the One who will get us out of it.** Yet the rescuing gift is not exactly parallel to the death-dealing sin. If one man's sin put crowds of people at the dead-end abyss of separation from God, just think what God's gift poured through one man, Jesus Christ, will do! **There's no comparison between that death-dealing sin and this generous, life-giving gift.** The verdict on that one sin was the death sentence; the verdict on the many sins that followed was this wonderful life sentence. If death got the upper hand through one man's wrongdoing, can you imagine the breathtaking recovery life makes, sovereign life, in those who grasp with both hands this wildly extravagant life-gift, this grand setting-everything-right, that the one man Jesus Christ provides?*
>
> Romans 5:14-17 MSG [Emphasis mine]

Most believers relate more to an expectation of trouble, the inevitability of sinning, general guilt, confusion, and self-criticism than they do to righteousness, justification, and the blessings of God. But this "in Christ" reality is incredible and powerful, and it's repeated in the Scriptures from beginning to end.

So what's the deal? Why are people sick? Why are we so prone to the negative? Why do more Christians identify with Adam than identify with Jesus? Why do they continually identify with death and darkness more than they identify with light and life? Many even think it's a form of humility to live in defeat. ***But this is not pleasing to God.*** It's a false humility rooted in ignorance of God's gift; it is in ignorance of His Word and will. Ignorance is not bliss! And yes, what you don't know can hurt you. God said that His people could be destroyed for a lack of knowledge (Hosea 4:6), and this deficit of knowledge is at an all-time high in the church today.

Bear in mind that **without faith, it is impossible to please God** (Hebrews 11:6). Our faith and trust must be wholly centered in the Word of God and the work of the cross. This only comes through the renewing of your mind to the promises of God, which allows the Holy Spirit to bring revelation of who you are **now** in Christ. Don't let yourself be comfortable with a fraudulent identity in Adam.

We must aggressively pursue God and recover all that Jesus purchased for us. We simply have not been taught the new creation realities about who we are, what we have, and what we can do in Christ. All these realities are meant to become part of our day-to-day experience as we learn to live by faith. As long as we identify more with Adam than with Christ, we're cancelling out all these benefits. That is why I constantly repeat this message to help us change our identity from Adam to Christ. We must mix faith with the Word of God that reveals our new identity and the blessings that come with it, knowing that God is trustworthy and faithful to perform what He has promised.

THE IMAGE OF GOD IN MAN

The triune God—Father, Son, and Holy Spirit—created a perfect man in a perfect triune image. He made man in His **plural** image—a spirit, having a soul (heart, mind, will, and emotions), and living in a body. He made man with all authority and dominion to exercise His power in the earth. We were not created to be run over by poverty, sickness, discouragement, or defeat. In man's original state of creation, we were designed to rule and reign over all things in life.

> *And God said, Let us make man in our image, after our likeness: and let them have dominion over the fish of the seas, and over the fowl of the air, and over the cattle, and over all the earth, and over every creeping thing that creepeth upon the earth.*
>
> Genesis 1:26 KJV

> *Man was created so much in the image of God that he was made just a little lower than God Himself.*

> *O Lord, our Lord, How excellent is Your name in all the earth, Who have set Your glory above the heavens! What is man that You are mindful of him, And the son of man that You visit him? For You have made him a little lower than the angels, And You have crowned him with glory and honor.*
>
> Psalm 8:1,4-5

The word angels used here is translated from the Hebrew word ELOHIM, which is the plural form of the name of God. To say it another way, man was made just a little lower than the triune God. He was given preeminence in the earth, everything else being put underneath Him. No other creature was given the honor Adam was given. In fact, man is created so much like God that he often gets the mistaken idea that he is God.

God's portrait is made of kindness, love, mercy, gentleness, holiness, righteousness, faithfulness, creativity, judgment, and a knowledge of self. That is just to name a few of the many good aspects of our identity in Christ. All of these character traits of God were in Adam at creation. God is God with a capital G, and He made man so much like Himself that He referred to us as gods with a little g in the Psalms.

> *Jesus answered them, "Is it not written in your law, 'I said, "You are gods"'? If He called them gods, to whom the word of God came (and the Scripture cannot be broken), do you say of Him whom the Father sanctified and sent into the world, 'You are blaspheming,' because I said, 'I am the Son of God'?"*

> John 10:34-36 [Emphasis mine]

> *I said, "You are gods, And all of you are children of the Most High...."*

> Psalm 82:6 [Emphasis mine]

I want to emphasize here that I did **not** say you and I are God. I'm too dumb to be God, and you're too smart to think that any of us could be God. I'm simply trying to show you through an undeniable cloud of witnesses what God says about His creation dwelling in the earth.

> *And we have known and believed the love that God has for us. God is love, and he who abides in love abides in God, and God in him. Love has been perfected among us in this: that we may have boldness in the day of judgment; **because as He is, so are we in this world.***

> 1 John 4:16-17 [Emphasis mine]

Notice that as Jesus is in this world, so are we. He's not talking about when we go to heaven. He's talking about right now, right here, present tense. As God is sovereign over all creation, so are we sovereign in this world. God, in His sovereignty, gave man dominion over the whole earth and told him to subdue it, making him a mini version of Himself, crowned with His glory and honor.

The heaven, even the heavens, are the Lord's; But the earth He has given to the children of men.

Psalm 115:16

For "the earth is the Lord's, and all its fullness.

Corinthians 10:26

How do we reconcile these two passages that seem to contradict? God has ownership of the planet, and He owns the cattle on a thousand hills. But He gave stewardship of the earth to man and man is to be ruler. That's why there is a day of judgment. All of us will have account for how we lived. We have a responsibility before God to take care of what He owns. As part of our stewardship, we can use our time, treasure, and talent either to glorify self or the devil or to further the glory of God and the building of His kingdom. That means we have to walk in the revelation of who we really are—in the Spirit, in the kingdom, right here, right now. Satan, through the tyranny of sin and man yielding to him, hijacked man's authority and perverted it for evil and harm. Satan stole Adam's God-given authority and used it against him and God.

Because man is made in God's likeness, he has dominion over the earth and the ability to choose which identity he will adopt—fallen Adam or risen Christ. Adam was to exercise his authority in partnership with God, working in union with Him to fill the earth with God's splendor and abundance. Sin not only broke that partnership but also solidified a paralyzing union between man and the god of this world (Satan). Instead of the earth being full of people glorifying God, it became full of people glorifying themselves, which is not very glorious. Adam lost all of God's power and authority. It was given over to Satan through sin, and thus the world became ruled by sin's negative consequences.

But through Christ, God created a new race—a "grace race"—which embodies the character traits of the Father, traits manifested in Jesus Christ. Jesus gives this new race exceedingly greater power than the "base race" Adam created through his rebellion. We have the freedom to become part of that grace race.

Once you accept Jesus' gift of salvation—your rescue—you can begin to exercise the dominion He has given you. You will find increasing prosperity in your relationships, in your insight, in your ability to navigate difficult situations, and in the outcome of the work of your hands. Abundant joy and understanding will spring up out of your heart. You will glorify God. God's character will show up in you and all the things around you will change. Your daily life will satisfy your heart in ways that were not possible when you lived with the perspective of "the old man"—the fallen Adam.

God has said, "With long life I will satisfy [you] and show [you] my salvation" (Psalm 91:16). The word translated here as *satisfy* is *sabea* (saw-bah), which means *fill to satisfaction, have enough, be full of, have plenty of, be satiated.* The word salvation used in this verse is the Hebrew Yeshua, which carries the hefty meanings of *deliverance, aid, victory, prosperity, health, help, and welfare.* All these are God-attributes. They are in the likeness of our heavenly Father. They are adjectives about our identity.

When you see that God has made provision for you to be restored to Him, and you choose to identify with Christ, your life will begin to display the breathtaking reality of the new creation. However, you must deliberately choose to identify with the attributes of Christ. This is the glory that displays the love and redemption of God to a lost and dying world. In Christ our authority to bind and loose in prayer has been fully restored (Matthew 18:18-20).

Every enemy is under our feet as we walk out our new identity. In Christ we have newfound authority over sin, sickness, poverty, and all the powers of darkness.

> *I can do all things **through Christ** [new identity] who strengthens me.*
> Philippians 4:13[Emphasis and brackets mine]

> *Now thanks be to God who **always leads us in triumph** in Christ, and through us diffuses the fragrance of His knowledge in every place.*
> 2 Corinthians 2:14 [Emphasis mine]

In the new creation, God is reversing the curse of the old creation in Adam. So, what is more real to you—sickness or healing? Poverty or prosperity? Sorrow or joy? In our day-to-day reality, sickness seems stronger than health, and depression seems stronger than joy. In our new reality in Christ, sickness is a firecracker, and healing is an atomic bomb. That bomb has already gone off in the enemies' camp. It went off in the resurrection.

CHAPTER NINE

IDENTITY VS. ROLES

One of the things I learned early in ministry was how to separate my identity in Christ from any station I occupied. For example, we all have different hats to wear—father, mother, teacher, boss, friend. I might be great as a teacher and not so great as a father, but my great performance as a teacher cannot increase the value of my identity, nor can my weakness as a father **decrease** my value. The point is, our identity in Christ is **a constant;** it never fluctuates. On a scale of one to ten, our performance on the job might be a six and our performance as a steward of our money might be a three, but our value in Christ is always ten. We can critique all the roles we have in life, but our identity is always perfect.

Most people are really messed up in this respect. Don't think I'm just putting other people down; I stand accused. I used to lead the pack! Now, because of my experience and security in Christ, I can really help people who struggle in this area if they will open their hearts and receive.

Much of the dysfunction people experience is because of how they perceive themselves. While many things over the years can contribute to this, none seems to have greater impact than how we perform in our occupation—from janitor to rocket scientist. The performance issue is always the same. If we think we're only as successful as the amount of money we make, how well we cook, what kind of house we live in, how good we are at making business deals, or anything else along those lines then we've fallen into a trap.

When your role and performance constitute your selfhood—when they're allowed to become your identity—you'll find yourself enslaved. You will constantly be in a position of comparing yourself to others and striving for approval.

For you to develop into a mature believer, it's important that you thoughtfully separate your identity from your role. As I said, your identity is stable, unwavering. It is eternal and secure in Christ. Your performance in different roles fluctuates depending on many different factors, some within your control and many more decidedly beyond it.

If you think what you do is who you really are, then you're in for a world of hurt. No matter how you strive for excellence in your job or social standing or how great your car is or how big your house is, you will end up living in a state of bondage that destroys the purpose of God in your life. If you think that **not** having those things makes you a failure, you are dead wrong.

More than that, if you think failing at something makes you a failure, you're accepting a lie. Failing is an event in the journey of life. Failure is not a permanent address (bad fallen identity). Think of a parent (a good one)—who loves his or her child beyond words. If that child just can't seem to learn math or is totally clumsy with a basketball, so what? That parent loves that kid for who he or she is—their beloved, wonderful child. Skills or no skills, that son or daughter is highly valued.

Failing at things we do is just a common part of life. No one is good at everything. Falling and failing and failing yet again is a part of the human condition.

> *For a just man falleth seven times, and riseth up again.*
> Proverbs 24:16 KJV

You may have failed at some things or even a lot of things, but that doesn't mean you are a failure. If your identity is in Jesus, you are a success. When God the Father is your parent, you have the ultimate cheerleader and the complete provider of all your esteem, value, and worth. In God's book, you are already perfected in your inner man, and your outer man will be able to continually grow up in God in all things. This means your performance in any given venue will continue to improve. I've failed many times over the years, but I'm not a failure in any sense of the word. In fact, my failing has become a blessing to others because of what God has taught me through the trials and challenges of life.

> *Blessed be the God and Father of our Lord Jesus Christ, the Father of mercies and God of all comfort, who comforts us in all our tribulation, that we may be able to comfort those who are in any trouble, with the comfort with which we ourselves are comforted by God.*
> 2 Corinthians 1:3-4

The Lord has taught me much from my mistakes; I've been healed and comforted by the Spirit. I've experienced His great love and mercy in forgiveness. I've received His instruction in wisdom and total restoration. I'm able to comfort others with the comfort I've received. I can teach them how to get back up again and continue in the purposes of God.

Jesus warned Peter of Satan's desire to sift him as wheat and said, "but I have prayed for you, that your faith should not fail; and when you have returned to *Me,* strengthen your brethren" (Luke 22:32). This is in reference to Peter denying the Lord three times before daybreak on the night of His arrest and mockery of a trial. Once Peter had failed and then recovered, he could help others who felt they had failed the Lord to get back up and move on. When we can be healed and forgiven of our mistakes, we can use them to be merciful to others who fall. Peter never forgot that weak moment, and because of it he was able to show mercy to others with the same weakness.

Imagine how the apostle Paul felt after he had received the revelation of Jesus. He had held the coats of the men who stoned Stephen, he had beaten and flogged people in the synagogues, and he had split families apart as he hauled men and women off to prison. Yet, in spite of these widely known facts, he wrote an astounding statement to the church at Corinth.

> *Receive us; we have wronged no man, we have corrupted no man, we have defrauded no man.*
>
> 2 Corinthians 7:2 KJV

How could Paul say he had wronged no one when he had such a history of violence? He could talk like that because he was a new man in Christ. He had a grip on his identity with the God of mercy. He did not look back, and he did not look at his everyday shortcomings.

> *Brethren, I do not count myself to have apprehended; but one thing I do, forgetting those things which are behind and*

reaching forward to those things which are ahead, I press toward the goal for the prize of the upward call of God in Christ Jesus.

Philippians 3:13-14

Paul did not allow his performance to affect who he was or the call he had on his life. After seeing how horrible his actions were, he could have chosen to fall apart or self-destruct through guilt and condemnation. Instead, he looked forward. He kept believing for the grace of God's empowering presence in his life, and he pressed to fulfill all that God had shown him.

When your identity becomes secure in Jesus, you can fix the failing part. It's important to get this perspective settled in your thinking because we all face falling short at some point or another. For instance, it is common knowledge that many men get depressed when they lose a job. They spiral downward in defeat and often become secretly hopeless because they thought of that job as something that defined them. Without it, they feel like nothing.

Men say things like, "I'm a corporate executive," or "I'm an electrician," or "I'm a software engineer." They become so connected with their work that when they're laid off or fired, they become less in their own eyes than what they were when they were working. We've got to turn this kind of thinking on its head! A man must not be defined by his work. Rather, **he** must define the work he does. Work does not make the man; the man makes the work what it is.

Because I am a child of God, I make work an act of worship, and in doing so, I am celebrating my uniqueness and contributing to my fellow man. Work then becomes a blessing to me and to others. I may lose my job, but I never lose who I am as created by the Father.

I never lose the gifts and callings He placed within me. My work is the overflow of who I am, not the source thereof.

> *But by the grace of God I am what I am: and his grace which was bestowed upon me was not in vain; but I laboured more abundantly than they all: yet not I, but the grace of God which was with me.*

1 Corinthians 15:10 KJV

Paul said he was who he was by grace, not by his role as an apostle. He went on to explain that his labor (what he did), came out of his identity by grace. Grace defines who all believers are, and what we do proceeds out of that same grace. My performance within any given role, any hat I wear—pastor, father, husband, brother, etc.—can improve. Yet, who I am cannot improve because it is a ten (on a one to ten scale) all the time in Jesus! That's amazing grace!

In the world's way of doing things, it's easy to get our feelings hurt; it's easy for pride to rear up. But we don't have to live that way. The spirit of God is in us. If my performance is not as great as I would like it to be, I don't have to take it personally. I know I'm still a perfect ten in God. Whatever I do, I do from the position of being a son of the King.

I listen for correction, knowing there is a positive outcome. I bring value to my work; my work does not bring value to me. I am who I am regardless of my employment status. Being a ten on a scale doesn't come from anything in the flesh. It comes as a free gift from the love of God. We haven't done a single thing to deserve it; we simply have been loved **beyond measure**.

For some, this may sound arrogant, but true arrogance is found in anyone who thinks he or she can attain holiness or perfection through his or her own efforts. It takes the power of the Holy Spirit to create a new inward man in us, to reveal all things and lead us into all truth. It takes true humility to accept by faith our new identity in Christ as a free gift (God's grace).

The Scripture clearly states that boasting in the flesh and self-righteousness are absolute arrogance, but if my boasting is in the finished work of the cross, then that is faith and genuine humility.

> *But God forbid that I should boast **except** in the cross of our Lord Jesus Christ, by whom the world has been crucified to me, and I to the world.*
>
> Galatians 6:14 [Emphasis mine]

> *For by grace you have been saved through faith, and that not of yourselves; it is the gift of God, not of works, lest anyone should boast.*
>
> Ephesians 2:8-9

MY ROLE AS HUSBAND

The day I got married, I was a ten in the eyes of my bride and in the eyes of God. After six weeks of marriage, I'm certain I dropped in Sue's eyes from a ten to about a three. (Okay...one and a half!) I was young, and I had no idea how to properly fulfill the role of husband. So if you judged me by my performance, I would land near the bottom of the scale. But years later, I'm much better at being a husband, and I'm not "one and a half" anymore! I may not be a ten yet (I believe I receive; I reach for the prize of the high calling...). But I can tell you this: Sue sure is glad she chose me. I have evolved from hamburger to prime rib. I'm pegging the needle at an eight on a consistent basis (Thank you, Jesus!).

MY ROLE AS PASTOR

As a pastor, I'm also not a ten. If my identity was wrapped up in pastoring and what everyone in my congregation thought of me, I'd be a train wreck waiting to happen—with casualties! I'd go down and take a lot of people down with me. I would probably be—no, scratch that—I would undoubtedly be depressed. I know some of my congregation would rate me as a three and others a four. Realistically, I think I pull off at least a six or seven. I strive for a perfect ten in my preaching, but it's certainly not a ten yet. It's a ten when it comes into my heart from the Holy Spirit and a ten before I open my mouth, but as soon as the words come out of my earthen vessel, the number begins to decrease. I stumble over sentences. I accidentally reverse things in my delivery. In many cases, I butcher the English language like a champion.

All that is to say if I don't keep seeing myself through the eyes of God, I could easily end up in a dysfunctional place. I could struggle in pastoring. But because I'm secure in my identity, I can evaluate and score my role with honesty and truthfulness, with no sense of having failed if I score low. I am not offended or defensive with my evaluation of these roles because they don't define who I am. Who I am is strong in God. Who I am will continually define and readjust my roles. In time, these adjustments will improve my score.

Not knowing the power of separating identity, role, and performance hinders the maturing process immensely. Yes, works (and how we perform) will amount to a very important part in the Christian life—just not in the area of our value and salvation. If only we can see the truth of our identity, everything else can line up properly and work well. Firstly, we are established in Christ, which is secure and constant. Secondly, we have hats to wear—roles to perform. Thirdly, we actually perform—we do well or not so well. But the primary thing is our establishment in Christ.

If I say to an employee, "You're not doing your job very well," he or she immediately feels that my opinion is a personal assessment of his or her value. The person thinks, *Brother Duane thinks I am no good.* That couldn't be further from the truth. I may think the job the person does is no good, but as a person he or she is precious in my sight. In the workplace, performance is important, and if I've hired a person to do a job, he or she must do it well.

I don't pay people based on who they are in Christ; I pay them to do a job and do it with excellence. They are saved by grace through faith, but they are paid by work and performance. If their performance is lacking, I still love them and believe in them, but something has to change. It could be as simple as discovering they are in the wrong position and would thrive in another area.

In our ministry, we call it the "seat on the bus"—a Jim Collin's concept from the book *Good to Great*. While we believe everyone God joins to our team is on the right bus, an employee may be in the wrong seat. Or, an employee may be in need of training to get the skill set required for his or her current position.

Whatever the case, if people gain the understanding that their personal value is a ten regardless of their performance in any given role, that will open the door of humility whereby they can receive the instruction and constructive criticism needed to improve. We all want to excel, so input ought to be welcomed.

> *I am the vine, you are the branches. He who abides in Me, and I in him, **bears much fruit**; for without Me you can do nothing.*
>
> John 15:5 [Emphasis mine]

> *By this My Father is glorified, that you **bear much fruit;** so you will be My disciples.*
>
> John 15:8 [Emphasis mine]

In the kingdom to come, we'll be rewarded according to our fruit or the good works produced as a byproduct of the root that's in us—Jesus. He is the vine; we are the branches. Branches bear fruit. It's important to note the difference between **bearing** fruit and **producing** it. Jesus produces the fruit; we simply bear it. All of our fruit is a byproduct of our relationship with Jesus, the true vine.

You are the head and not the tail in Jesus. You are above and not beneath, blessed coming in and blessed going out. You are the seed of Abraham, a king and a priest, ruling and reigning in the earth. You are complete in Jesus. This is your new identity. Once you get this settled in your whole heart and sell out to it completely, your actions will start changing supernaturally from the inside out. Once you behold this truth—and you're being "held" by it—the fruit in your life will begin to line up with the Spirit who's in you.

We need to recognize who we are and improve our actions through believing in the power that comes from our identity in Christ. This is how we bear much fruit to the glory of God.

Jesus is Lord. We are His. Let's act like it.

2/10/21

CHAPTER TEN

BEING VS. DOING

When an orange tree is just a sapling, only a few feet high, it has no oranges on it. But don't we still call it an orange tree? We know with its root system down in the ground drawing up nutrients, the oranges are surely going to come in time. Nobody looks at it on the day the oranges appear and says, "This tree just became an orange tree today." It was an orange tree all along; the fruit simply bears witness to the true nature of the tree.

Why then do Christians seem to think it's their fruit—their good works—that make them a good or bad Christian? The fruit in the Christian life does not make us anything. We are a new creation the minute we get saved. If we stay rooted and grounded in the Word, the fruit of the Spirit will come onto our tree in time and be a blessing to the world around us.

> *As you therefore have received Christ Jesus the Lord, so walk in Him, **rooted and built up in Him** and established in the faith, as you have been taught, abounding in it with thanksgiving.*
>
> Colossians 2:6-7 [Emphasis mine]

BEING VS. DOING (ALL THE RIGHT STUFF)

> *Do you not know that the unrighteous will not inherit the kingdom of God? Do not be deceived. Neither fornicators, nor idolaters, nor adulterers, nor homosexuals, nor sodomites, nor thieves, nor covetous, nor drunkards, nor revilers, nor extortioners will inherit the kingdom of God. **And such were some of you**. But you were washed, but you were sanctified, but you were justified in the name of the Lord Jesus and by the Spirit of our God.*
>
> 1 Corinthians 6:9-11 [Emphasis mine]

Under the inspiration of the Holy Spirit, the apostle Paul made it emphatically clear we **were** these things as opposed to **being** them in the present. God no longer sees you in that light. Rather, He sees you as He has declared you to be in His new creation.

You **are** washed. You **are** sanctified. You **are** justified.

We used to be all the wrong stuff (in Adam), but now we are **all the right stuff** (in Christ). We acted like we acted because that was who we were—just as a dog barks because he's a dog. But as born-again believers, we're not the same as our old selves. We're changed, so our actions need to change.

My point is, there's a huge difference between **being** a sinner, i.e., an adulterer, and **being** a washed, sanctified, and justified believer tempted with adultery. A believer may even fall into committing the sin, but that in no way makes him an adulterer. The believer is new in his born-again nature in Christ. Now, as a faithful brother, I can admonish my fellow believer in the love and words of the Lord, "Put off the old man!" I can tell him to repent for the act of adultery because that's not who he is in Christ.

For another example, consider a thief. A person can go from his old identity in Adam that takes from others unlawfully to a new identity in Christ where he becomes a servant. As a believer comes to know who he is in God, he forgoes the temptation to steal and begins giving to others.

> *Let him who stole steal no longer, but rather let him labor, working with his hands what is good, that he may have something to give him who has need.*
>
> Ephesians 4:28

But even if a believer who used to be a thief falls into a temptation, he is still not made a thief again. He remains a new creation, and he can repent and pick himself up in his new identity. There is a difference in **being** and **doing**. If you are by nature a thief, then stealing is a byproduct of who you are. You can't help what you do if that's who you are in Adam. But **in** Christ, you are a new creation—a servant. If you steal something, you need to repent and turn from that because it is not who you are in Jesus.

How about bad thoughts? Have you had any bad thoughts since you were saved? I have. I've even had bad thoughts while preaching, especially when I've looked over the crowd. (Come on! You can laugh at that one for sure!) Since we all have bad thoughts, does that mean we're bad people? Do you see how important it is to separate identity from thoughts, actions, and even feelings?

Feelings are very real, and that's how offense comes. But feelings are also majorly unreliable. Sometimes I feel unworthy. Does that mean I am unworthy? No, God has made me worthy. I must separate my true self from my feelings by taking every thought captive and bringing it into the obedience of Jesus Christ. The feelings will eventually change, just like my thoughts and actions change as I mature. These things no longer control me; I control them through my new man. I'm now the master in submission to the senior master, Jesus.

Have you ever failed at a job? Have you ever lied? Christians are not failures or liars by nature, but you and I both have all fallen at one time or another into this insidiousness. Have you lied since you've known the Lord? Be honest! I may lose a measure of respect in my honesty, but I can tell you that I've committed this sin even after I was saved. Early in my Christian walk, I told a lie because I was scared and intimidated. I was under pressure, and I thought I would get rejected. Then, the coolest thing happened. Because being a liar is no longer my nature in Christ, I was very uncomfortable with that lie and felt horribly convicted.

You might wonder how I could be happy about feeling horrible, but that experience showed me who I really am. It showed me that I'm not a liar, and I'm not comfortable in any way telling lies. It showed me that this was just not the real me. I decided, So what if they reject me? *So what if everything blows up? I can't live with lying because that's not who I am anymore. I'll just go back and repent to them.* So I did. I repented, and it was awesome! I was free as a bird, all condemnation was gone. They actually respected my honesty.

I use this as an example to help people. Don't misunderstand me. I haven't lied recently, and I don't condone lying. I'm just making the point that the poor choice I made did not make me a liar by nature and failing at something does not make a Christian a loser. Because of my new identity in Christ, I can put away "lying one to another" (Colossians 3:9-10; Ephesians 4:24-25). I don't want to be associated with liars because the Word says they will all have their place in the lake of fire with the false prophet, the harlot church, and the national media (Okay, maybe I went a little too far there. My sentiments sneak out here and there because the continual lying and propaganda disguised as "news" is an issue with me and millions of other people. But that's a subject for another time, so stay tuned!).

Paul's extensive list in Second Corinthians 6:9-11 shows our fallen condition and identity in Adam of which Christ has washed and cleansed us. We're not these things "in Christ" any longer, even if we struggle with them after the flesh. Let's reveal them again because those who choose to be these things in Adam will not inherit the kingdom of God. Notice again the difference between **being** and **doing**.

> *Don't you realize that those who do wrong will not inherit the kingdom Of God? Don't fool yourselves. Those who indulge in sexual sin, or who worship idols, or commit adultery, or are male prostitutes, or practice homosexuality, or are thieves, or greedy people, or drunkards, or are abusive, or cheat people—none of these will inherit the kingdom of God.*
>
> 1 Corinthians 6:9-10 NLT

Wow! That's an extensive list, and it's made pretty clear. It lists ten specific conditions in Adam that are sinful, selfish, and destructive. None of these are good or healthy, nor do they show love toward God, ourselves, or our fellow man. Verse 11 goes on to say: "**Some of you were once like that.** But you were cleansed; you were made holy; you were made right with God by calling on the name of the Lord Jesus Christ and by the Spirit of our God" (NLT). This is who we were in Adam and that which we are no longer because we are in Christ. These things were not just things we did, but who we were. Now we are no longer these things, so put them away. Walk away from acting like you did when you were in Adam. Act differently because now you are in Christ. In the world, we would say, "Be real. Be yourself." Those in Christ say, "Be like Him. Be Christlike."

I have no ill will toward anyone who is in bondage of any kind—from the least to the worst of unspeakable acts. But the truth must be spoken in love because there's no end to the black hole of depravity. The only destroyer of darkness is the light of God. And the only enemy of light is silence.

> *Let your light so shine before men, that they may see your good works and glorify your Father in heaven.*
>
> Matthew 5:16

All sin is unrighteous behavior that harms people. God isn't against sin because He doesn't want us to enjoy life. He's against it because He knows these engagements will wreck us and wreck others around us. He knows what it does to the culture—nothing good! Our culture can barely even stand to use the word *sin,* and they put a lot of energy into making sin look enticing and fun. However, the fact is that sin only offers a phony happiness. It's pleasurable only for a season, and it always ends in ugliness, pain, and misery. As Christians, we may still struggle with sin, but we know it's not who we are and does not define us. We are able to walk out of it in the power that has been deposited in us in Christ.

God created man for greatness and a life full of beauty and joy. As righteous children of God, we have the ability to flee from sin that drags us down.

> *For this is the will of God, your sanctification: that you should abstain from sexual immorality; that each of you should know how to possess his own vessel in sanctification and honor.*
>
> 1 Thessalonians 4:3-4

Flee sexual immorality. Every sin that a man does is outside the body, but he who commits sexual immorality sins against his own body.

1 Corinthians 6:18

In Oklahoma talk, flee means, Feet, don't fail me now! Put on your Nikes and run for the hills! Make the decision to run the other way while you renew your mind. Know that over time, God's Word will make you free from entering temptation and that which is harmful to you. It will lead you to a whole new view of yourself, one that lines up word for word with God's thoughts.

"JUST LOVE"

I've heard it said, "We just need to love people, and that will set them free." No, it absolutely will not! We do need to love people and be kind and compassionate to everyone—no matter what weakness of the flesh they struggle with or where they are in life. But the Scriptures say it's knowing the truth of God's Word that sets people free.

We must speak the truth in love for people to be saved from iniquity and trouble. His Word will not only make you free from what is harmful to you, but also it will lead you into a whole new view of yourself. It will lead you to a God view that actually lines up word for word with Scripture and becomes effectual, showing up by visible results in your life. That is the whole point of understanding your identity in Christ. You let it become a revelation, so you can act like who you are: more than a conqueror over strife, sickness, lack, and all manner of the things that plague a godless world.

Sanctify them by Your truth. Your word is truth.

John 17:17

> *Jesus said to the people who believed in him, "You are truly my disciples if you remain faithful to my teachings. And you will know the truth, and the truth will set you free."*
>
> John 8:31-32 NLT

It's the truth, spoken in love, that breaks the deception and power of sin. God's Word is truth. It's the only thing that can set us free and keep us free. This is also how we're to bring up our little ones—with a clear presentation of the truth. I never want to embarrass any of my children, but some of the things that have happened in our family are just classics. Please understand that I mean well when I tell these stories, as I'm certain they will help others. When my daughter, Shekinah, was about eight or nine, she disobeyed and needed to "be loved" the way the Bible says that a child should be loved in his or her upbringing.

> *He who spares his rod hates his son, But he who **loves him disciplines him** promptly.*
>
> Proverbs 13:24 [Emphasis mine]

> *Foolishness is bound up in the heart of a child; The rod of **correction** will drive it far from him.*
>
> Proverbs 22:15 [Emphasis mine]

The New Testament says those whom the Lord loves, He rebukes and chastens. This is true just as we have had fathers of our flesh correct us in order to bring about the peaceable fruit of righteousness. And on this particular occasion, Shekinah certainly had some foolishness in her heart that needed to be driven out.

I want to add that a good father does not provoke his children to wrath with the rod of **punishment**, but rather raises them in the nurture and admonition of the Lord with the rod of **correction**. **There's** a huge difference! A rod of punishment is wrath, anger, and a selfish motive invoked on a child. It could be a form of child abuse on multiple levels—physical, emotional, or psychological. The rod of correction, however, is loving accountability which carries consequences. This rod is invoked in sincere concern for the child and his or her well-being. It's also a rod that helps a child identify with the attributes of their heavenly Father. The rod of correction defines boundaries early in the child's development, creating an understanding of pain associated with sin (disobedience) as well as an understanding of God's perspective on things. The pain of loving discipline is not to be compared to a life of pain in prison because one never learned the consequences of selfish behavior.

As another example of the merciful rod of correction, a four-year-old who wants to continually run out into the street does not have the capacity to visualize why it's dangerous. But the child certainly does have the capacity to visualize an immediate (but actually harmless) pain that mama will inflict if they go out the front door and into the street. This restrains them. This helps them. It is all about viewpoint—God's viewpoint, specifically.

If I truly love my children, I will chasten or discipline them early in life concerning the way they should go. They should go toward who they are in God, and the Word promises they will not depart from it. So, concerning my daughter, Shekinah, love just overtook me. I ministered to her by applying "love" through appropriate discipline to her gluteus maximus. At first, when I simply tried to talk to her about right and wrong, she got dramatic on me. She's the most dramatic of all my children, and she just fell apart.

She started crying, wailing, and bawling, "I just can't do right. I am soooo bad! I just need to die and go to hell!"

"Shekinah," I said, "It's just a spanking."

Some people reading this may actually have never heard of a spanking before. In our culture, it seems to have become something of myth and legend. But I'm talking about a S-P-A-N-K-I-N-G: A time-tested method of discipline in which an object held in the hand (in my house, a wooden spoon called "Mr. Spoon") is applied with laser precision to the fat seat of the child. It causes a signal to be sent to the brain, which causes synapses to fire, which causes tear ducts to open, at which point a bolt of lightning strikes the child's brain and brings him or her to a resolve to never to do that piece of stupid again. That's the definition of *SPANKING* by Duane Sheriff.

"Shekinah," I said, "You might feel like it for a moment, but you're not going to die. And you're certainly not going to hell because you've already given your life to Christ."

Shekinah was saved, and we knew that beyond any shadow of a doubt. So I looked at her and said, "Shekinah, look at me. You're not a bad person. You're a good person [her identity]. Your name is Shekinah. God gave me your name, and it means *the glory of God*. You're going to have an impact on this world, and you're going to make a difference! You are very good! You are awesome! Now, start acting like it!"

I can't count the number of times I've looked at the church and said, "Don't you know who you are? You're not bad, you're good! You're not unrighteous. You're the very righteousness of God. Now start acting like it!"

Sometime later, Shekinah was in dire need of love again. And since I was compelled to save her from foolishness, destruction, and self-centeredness (yes, another meeting with "Mr. Spoon") she had the "fall-aparts." She started to cry and said, "I just can't do it! I can't obey! I just want to die and go to heaven!" At least her theology had improved. She had changed. Unfortunately, I realized that I had changed a bit too because when I first looked at her I thought, *I'm about ready to send you to heaven....* But I held my tongue and resisted my impulses. Now don't judge me on this; I'm just being honest. We've all had those moments when we hit the end of our rope and start thinking things like, *Can't we just be done with this?! The kids are driving me crazy!*

It's a scientific fact that spiders eat their young, and I'm certain that the spirit of a spider has come upon all parents at one time or another. However, we know it's best to exercise restraint and maturity, not taking any disciplinary action in an emotional state, especially a state of anger. The point I'm trying to make is that early on, I had to teach my children to separate their identification from their actions and feelings. I gave them the whole list: You are good, but what you did was bad. You are righteous, but that is unrighteous. You are holy in God, sealed in your inner man, but what you did is from your old man. You have to put that off and put this on.

We all can get wobbly in areas of weakness, yet we are empowered by God's grace to overcome any bad thoughts, negative emotions, and sinful actions that violate our new condition. Jesus, the pattern Son, demonstrated that we are indeed able to overcome these temptations that seem to take people out of the race so readily.

> *For we do not have a High Priest who cannot sympathize with our weaknesses, but was in all points tempted as we are, yet without sin.*
>
> Hebrews 4:15

> *Since he himself has gone through suffering and testing, he is able to help us when we are being tested.*
>
> Hebrews 2:18 NLT

Just because a person is tempted with sin or self-deprecating thoughts doesn't mean he has sinned. That would imply that Jesus Himself sinned because of a temptation, and we all know better than that. Satan tempts us through our thoughts and emotions in order to get us to doubt God just like Adam did in the garden. But we don't have to act it out. We must simply learn to submit ourselves to God and to resist the devil. When we do, he will flee. It is commanded that he must flee from us (James 4:7).

> *Let no one say when he is tempted, "I am tempted by God"; for God cannot be tempted by evil, nor does He Himself tempt anyone. But each one is tempted when he is drawn away by his own desires and enticed. Then, when desire has conceived, it gives birth to sin; and sin, when it is full-grown, brings forth death.*
>
> James 1:13-15

The book of Revelation says we overcome Satan **by the blood of the Lamb and the word of our testimony.** The blood of the Lamb is the sacrificial price Jesus paid in full to save us from our sins and all the repercussions, damages, and negatives of sin in life. That is why Second Corinthians 1:20 says all the promises are yes and amen in Christ Jesus.

The word of our testimony is the believer's spoken confession that Jesus is the Lord who ensures our victory. We overcome sin by identifying with Jesus and the finished work of the cross. We do not overcome sin by identifying with it. As believers, we may still sin (fall short), but we never **become** that sin.

In the world, there are programs that help people manage their sin, but they do not make a way for us to be free from sin. People who struggle with alcoholism are taught to get up every day and confess,

"I am an alcoholic." Through certain steps, they are able to manage and control their drinking problems. While I don't doubt some people have been helped, they are not free. It's not freedom to have to identify with sin in Adam. It's not freedom to confess and believe you're an alcoholic the rest of your life. In Christ, you are righteous and truly holy, and in identifying with Jesus, the grace of God breaks the dominion of any bondage.

Satan keeps us bound by sin through **deceiving us into believing we are our sin.** If you're a born-again believer who has a drinking problem, you're not an alcoholic! You're a child of the King, the one true God, endued with power from on high to overcome your drinking problem. You have a weakness in your flesh that Satan exploits to draw you away from God and your dependency on Him. That's the old man who must be put off. How? By putting on the new man. How? By the renewing of your mind to your **new identity in Christ.**

You're a new person inside who still has weakness on the outside.

It's your new identity in Jesus (not sin) that breaks the power of any weakness of your flesh. The Word tells us to speak His Word about who we are—out loud—in order to help us walk in the revelation of our identity with Christ.

> *That the sharing of your faith may become effective by the acknowledgment of every good thing which is in you in Christ Jesus.*
>
> Philemon 1:6

We need to learn to confess who we are in Christ and all the good within us, applying this in both our successes and our failures. As Christians, when it comes to sin, we either need to be delivered or discipled in the Word. If it's a true demonic problem, it needs to be cast out because demons can't be discipled. If it's a weakness in the flesh, a stronghold, it needs to be pulled down through the Word of God and the words of your mouth. The power of life and death is in the tongue. Unfortunately, we can't simply cast out flesh; we need to learn to put its deeds or works to death.

We simply need to be discipled in the truth. We need to follow the direction of the Holy Spirit, open our mouths, and speak the Word of God to our mountains. If you struggle in this area, you need to realize you're no longer a drunkard or an alcoholic. You're a Christian. You're an heir of God and a joint-heir with Jesus. Satan may tempt you with alcohol or other situations, but you can overcome the temptation because **you can do all things through Christ who strengthens you.** Seize the opportunity to live the life Jesus paid for you to live.

The best of you—Christ in you—can now rule the rest of you through the renewing of your mind.

Confess and learn to believe who you are in Christ, not any weakness of your flesh. Confess the Word because you are a branch of the best fruit tree in the universe—the true vine, Jesus Christ (John 15:1).

2/17/21

CHAPTER ELEVEN
SPIRIT, SOUL, & BODY

Part of being who God says you are is understanding that you're a three-part being created in His image—spirit, soul, and body. We cannot experience the reality of who we are in Christ without knowing how the three parts of our existence function in the earth and in the spiritual realm. When we accept Jesus, our spirit is changed, but our brains, emotions, and body have to get in line with the change. They have to learn how to live according to the work done in our spirit. In Scripture, we can readily see that we are three parts.

> *Now may the God of peace Himself sanctify you completely; and may your whole **spirit, soul, and body** be preserved blameless at the coming of our Lord Jesus Christ. He who calls you is faithful, who also will do it.*
> 1 Thessalonians 5:23-24 [Emphasis mine]

Then we have to wrap our minds around the fact that some part of us is absolutely new.

> *Therefore, if anyone is in Christ, he is a **new creation**; old things have passed away; behold, **all things have become new.***
>
> 2 Corinthians 5:17 [Emphasis mine]

In simple terms, this means all things become new in our spirit, and we are wall-to-wall Jesus on the inside. Our spirit is born of the Spirit and is one with the Lord (1 Corinthians 6:17).

In John 3:6, Jesus speaks of flesh producing nothing but flesh, and spirit producing nothing but spirit. Whatever the Holy Spirit is, your spirit is born of that. This is an astounding thing to contemplate, mostly because we live so far below the reality of God's power available in our lives.

In some scriptures, man is defined as a two-part being, having an inward man and an outer man. In other scriptures, man is described as a three-part being—spirit, soul, and body. So, you might ask, "Which one is it? Two parts or three parts?"

We can see in the Word of God that the inner man is the heart, which is the combination of spirit and soul, while the outer man is the body. When you put these together, it's easy to see that the whole of man is actually the sum of all three parts—spirit, soul, and body.

> *Now may the God of peace Himself sanctify you completely; and may **your whole spirit, soul, and body** be preserved blameless at the coming of our Lord Jesus Christ.*
>
> 1 Thessalonians 5:23 [Emphasis mine]

THE SIMPLE BREAKDOWN OF THE SPIRIT, SOUL, AND BODY

1. THE SPIRIT

The spirit is the part of the heart immediately changed the moment you call upon the name of the Lord. First Peter 3:4 calls our spirit the "hidden man of the heart" and declares when we become renewed in God's Spirit, it's not "corruptible" (KJV). When we believe and give our hearts to Jesus, God supernaturally removes our hard heart and replaces it with **His** kind of heart—a soft and responsive heart.

> *And I will give them one heart [a new heart] and put a new spirit within them. I will take from them the heart of stone and will give them a heart of flesh [that is responsive to My touch].*
>
> Ezekiel 11:19 AMP

When you believe, things happen on the inside of you. They are accomplished in your spirit:

God puts a new spirit within you. The eternal part of you that is born again is born of the Spirit of God, and your eyes are opened to see the kingdom of God (John 3:3).

- Your spirit is saved by grace through faith in the work of Jesus at the cross. It is a gift from God (Ephesians 2:8).

- Your spirit becomes a new creation, and it's the only part of you that becomes new instantly (2 Corinthians 5:17).

- Your spirit is given the mind of Christ (1 Corinthians 2:16).

- Your spirit is one spirit with the Lord (1 Corinthians 6:17).

- Your Father God causes your spirit to be recreated in righteousness and true holiness (Ephesians 4:24).

- Your spirit is sealed unto the day of redemption (2 Corinthians 1:22; Ephesians 1:13; 4:30).

2. THE SOUL

The soul is the part of the heart being saved day by day—regenerated through the renewing of the mind by God's Word and the illumination of His Spirit. The soul refers to the mind, will, and emotions.

- The soul is changed as you behold God's glory—His character and purposes (2 Corinthians 3:18).

- The soul is a part of the inward man. Through your maturing in the Word of God, the soul puts off the old man. The soul also puts on the new man of the born-again spirit, created in righteousness and true holiness (Ephesians 4:22-24; 2 Corinthians 4:16).

- The soul is a part of the inner man, but it's so miraculously and intimately connected to your spirit that its thoughts can only be discerned and rightly divided by the Word of God (Hebrews 4:12).

- The soul can be carnally minded or spiritually minded (Romans 8:6).

- As the soul is renewed, it facilitates your transformation (Romans 12:2).

3. THE BODY

The body is your "earth suit" that allows you to live and exercise your God-given dominion over all the earth. Unless you're a teenager, you've probably figured out by now that this is the part of you that doesn't seem to be moving in a positive direction (Just look at your high school pictures!). This is the part of you who will be saved at the appearing of Jesus and His kingdom (in the resurrection, at the last day). The body is the purchased possession that has not yet been redeemed and is subject to weakness, mortality, and corruption. (Ephesians 1:13-14).

- The body is the part of you that's perishing and will be returned to the dust from which it's taken (2 Corinthians 4:16).

- If you're born again and your body is dead at the appearing of Jesus and His kingdom, it will rise first (before those living), and become an incorruptible, immortal body (1 Corinthians 15:51-54).

- For those who are alive and remain, the body will be changed in the twinkling of an eye. It will be caught up together with the others in the clouds to meet the Lord in the air. And so shall we ever be with the Lord (1 Thessalonians 4:16-17).

- The body is saved by hope—future tense:

> *We believers also groan, even though we have the Holy Spirit within us as a foretaste of future glory, for we long for our bodies to be released from sin and suffering. We, too, wait with eager hope for the day when God will give us our full rights as his adopted children, including **the new bodies** he has promised us. We were given this hope when we were saved. (If we already have something, we don't need to hope for it. But if we look forward to something we don't yet have, we must wait patiently and confidently.)*
>
> Romans 8:23-25 NLT [Emphasis mine]

For we know that if our earthly house, this tent, is destroyed, we have a building from God, a house not made with hands, eternal in the heavens. For in this we groan, earnestly desiring to be clothed with our habitation which is from heaven, if indeed, having been clothed, we shall not be found naked. For we who are in this tent groan, being burdened, not because we want to be unclothed, but further clothed, that mortality may be swallowed up by life. Now He who has prepared us for this very thing is God, who also has given us the Spirit as a guarantee. So we are always confident, knowing that while we are at home in the body we are absent from the Lord. For we walk by faith, not by sight. We are confident, yes, well pleased rather to be absent from the body and to be present with the Lord.

2 Corinthians 5:1-8

God's Word paints many pictures of the concept of spirit, soul, and body, but none can match the impact of the scriptures that describe the Temple of God in the Old Testament.

Regardless of whether it was the tabernacle of Moses or David, or Solomon's temple building, it was a holy place, which is how God sees us in Jesus. Now we are His holy place! Today, Jesus Christ has made us all kings and priests in temples not made with hands. We reside in the temples of our bodies, and He dwells within us.

YOU ARE THE TEMPLE OF GOD

The New Testament explains everything that the Old Testament contains, and the significance of God's temple is no exception. First and Second Corinthians are very explicit about it:

> *Do you not know that you are the temple of God and that the Spirit of God dwells in you? If anyone defiles the temple of God, God will destroy him. For the temple of God is holy, which temple you are.*
>
> 1 Corinthians 3:16-17

> *And what union can there be between God's temple and idols? For we are the temple of the living God. As God said: "I will live in them and walk among them. I will be their God, and they will be my people."*
>
> 2 Corinthians 6:16 NLT

This is who you are right now. This is not talking about some age to come. Solomon's temple was comprised of three distinct parts. It had an outer court and an inner court. On the inside of the inner court, there was an inner temple, which had two distinct chambers. These were the holy place and the most holy place. Each part of that temple relates to the parts of our temple—our being.

THE OUTER COURT—THE BODY

Our physical bodies are essentially the outer court of our temple, which gives us access to and authority in the world. This is the part that allows us to interact with others in a physical earth, so we may evangelize. This is where sin works, and thus, we must offer our bodies as a "living sacrifice" to God on a daily basis (Romans 12:1). Our bodies and being in our bodies are what give us authority on this earth. Once we leave our bodies (death), we no longer have physical authority.

No good thing resides in our flesh, but by faith we reckon our bodies dead to sin. However, we remain aware and alive unto God, yielding our bodies to Christ and His will (Romans 6, 7).

THE INNER COURT—THE SOUL

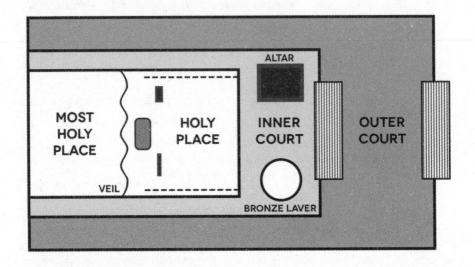

The inner court contained the bronze laver and altar. The laver was for the priests to continually wash their hands, which was a symbol of their need to be cleansed by the Word of God—a recognition that whatever God said was right. The fire on the altar was kept burning at all times, and daily sacrifices were offered morning and afternoon. It was a specifically appointed place to offer sacrifices for their shortcomings and to make special offerings and worship, honoring God's Almighty power and righteousness. There were holy things present but also unholy things that needed to be purified—cleansed with reverence, prayer, and the declaration of God's Word. This is a direct reference to the soul—to the thoughts, will, and emotions of the believer. These all need purification. This is where the issues of each individual are dealt with by the Spirit of God and His Word. It's where thoughts are purged and made clear and precise. Sanctification means we are unburdened and redeemed from a fallen nature, and we have become able to have emotions that are properly harnessed and brought into harmony with the truth and goodness of God. This is the part of the heart being saved **day by day**, purified by the washing of the water of the Word (Ephesians 5:26; 2 Corinthians 4:16).

The soul is the part of you that can join with your renewed spirit and overcome the flesh. Or, it can join with your flesh and overcome your spirit, thereby cancelling out or hindering all the promises of God. Jesus demonstrated this principle with His disciples at His last supper with them:

> *[Jesus] rose from supper and laid aside his garments, took a towel and girded Himself. After that, He poured water into a basin and began to wash the disciples' feet, and to wipe them with the towel with which He was girded.*
>
> *Then He came to Simon Peter. And Peter said to Him, "Lord, are You washing my feet?" Jesus answered and said to him, "What I am doing you do not understand now, but you will know after this." Peter said to Him, "You shall never wash my feet!"*
>
> *Jesus answered, him, "If I do not wash you, you have no part with me." Simon Peter said to Him, "Lord, not my feet only, but my hands and my head!" Jesus said to him, "He who is bathed needs only to wash his feet, but is completely clean; and you are clean, but not all of you."*
>
> John 13:4-10

Jesus was showing Peter and the other disciples the only part that needs to be cleansed in the believer's life is the part that touches the earth. It is the soul that touches the world through the body/mind connection, and therefore, the soul is the only part of your inner man that needs to be washed. This is done with the pure water of the Word. The Spirit side of your inner man is sealed unto the day of redemption and nothing of the world can penetrate it. The more the soul is renewed to the truth of God, the more you'll be able to align it with the spirit, overcoming everything the enemy tries to steal from you.

Only the soul and body are affected by sin. Your spirit has been renewed and has power. The spirit is righteous from the inside out, and it's worth repeating that nothing unrighteous or unholy can come from it or enter into it. God has forgiven us of all our sins. All sins truly means *ALL* sins, including past, present, future. And all our forgiveness is completely accomplished through the atonement of the cross. This is a wonderful gift.

Many people have not rightly divided the Word of Truth that explains the reason for New Testament repentance, which is a way of living out who we are in Christ.

If I make a mistake or do a piece of stupid, I am convicted over that because that's just not who I am in Christ. I am no longer at home or comfortable with sin—I come home to God in **receiving my forgiveness.**

On God's end, our forgiveness is a settled issue. It's true that Jesus paid the price with one sacrifice for sins forever. He permanently reconciled and secured our relationship with the Father. On our end, however, the deadliness of sin leaves us in a not-so-settled state. When we sin (and we all do), we're made vulnerable and insecure. Sin hurts us and often affects those around us as well. It not only corrupts the conscience but also causes self-condemnation and a lack of confidence in our relationship with God. Repentance is God's solution to that. God never condemns us over sin; it's our own heart that condemns us. While God convicts and corrects us for sin, it's always out of His love for us rather than out of wrath or anger. God convicts us of any sin in order to cleanse us of it and minimize the effects and consequences. Repentance is literally the key that unlocks the door to receiving an unashamed relationship with our heavenly Father.

> *For if the blood of bulls and goats and the ashes of a heifer, sprinkling the unclean, sanctifies for the purifying of the flesh, how much more shall the blood of Christ, who through the eternal Spirit offered himself without spot to God, cleanse your conscience from dead works to serve the living God?*
>
> Hebrews 9:13-14

The purpose of Christian repentance is not to attain unto something holy and righteous. We've already been made righteous by the blood of the lamb. This righteousness is a permanent condition in our spirit man, and it's one that never changes or leaves. Repentance simply purges a burdened conscience—it cleanses us supernaturally so we can stand with boldness before God without guilt or condemnation. It reminds us that our Father has paid all the bills that sin charges. Our repentance allows us to reject guilt and condemnation by taking away the power of sin that inhibits our ability to fellowship with Him. When we harbor sin, our thoughts and feelings get something like a fog over them, and our spiritual ears can become dull. It's almost as if there's static on the line. Repentance is a refreshing that clears the way for our spiritual hearing and confidence in our conversation with God. Keep in mind that the conscience, which is affected by sin, is a part of the soul, not the spirit. It's still at the renewal stage.

> *For if our heart condemns us, God is greater than our heart, and knows all things. Beloved, if our heart does not condemn us, we have confidence toward God.*
>
> 1 John 3:20-21

> *If we claim we have no sin, we are only fooling ourselves and not living in the truth. But if we confess our sins to him, he is faithful and just to forgive us our sins and to cleanse us from all wickedness.*
>
> 1 John 1:8-9 NLT

We receive forgiveness and cleansing from the effects and consequences of sin in our soul and body. It's important to stop sinning, but not for the reason many people think. God doesn't want you to stop sinning because He's dogmatic about a bunch of rules.

He's not angrily waiting for you to step out of line, so He can yank the slack out of you. He wants you to stop sinning because it's killing you. Sin not only affects your relationships with people; it impacts your relationship with Satan as well. **Yes! You have a relationship with Satan.** It can be one where you are perpetually at war with him, taking the power of the cross into battle against him every day. Or, it can be a relationship where you allow him to steal, kill, and destroy every good and perfect gift that comes down from the Father of lights. Satan and sin work disintegration into every area of your life, but obedience to the truth of the Word works in God's righteousness, blessings, good fortune, and increase. Sin gives a defeated devil an unnecessary opening into our lives. He takes advantage of that, using those doorways to destroy us.

> *Do you not know that to whom you present yourselves slaves to obey, you are that one's slaves whom you obey, whether of sin leading to death, or of obedience leading to righteousness?*
>
> Romans 6:16

Repentance isn't a tool to get God to love and accept you. It does not earn blessings. He cannot love you anymore than He does at this very moment. He cannot bless you with any more than He has already given. He swore a covenant oath that He would never leave or forsake you. In other words, you cannot do enough good to make Him love you any more than He already does, and you cannot be bad enough to make Him love you less. Repentance is merely the catalyst that allows you to receive the forgiveness that was provided by Jesus at the cross. We need repentance because our soul touches this world and is sullied by it. But keep it straight—your spirit is perfect. In essence, when we repent, Jesus is washing our feet. He's cleansing the part that walks the earth, the part that touches this present world and is impacted by sin and death.

THE INNER TEMPLE—A COMBINATION OF CHRIST'S SPIRIT AND OUR SPIRIT

The inner temple was the most sanctified place of all and was exclusively reserved for members of the priesthood. A thick veil separated two chambers (the Holy Place and the Most Holy Place), which only the high priest could enter so he could commune with the manifested presence of God. When Jesus died and the veil was ripped from top to bottom, this was a picture of God connecting you with Jesus for all eternity. That tearing of the veil signifies a new and living way had been made into the holiest of all. Notice it was from top to bottom, forever revealing it was God who did this—not man. Salvation is a **work of God and grace**, not man and works. This is where our individual spirit was inexplicably and marvelously united with the Spirit of Christ at the new birth, allowing us to enter the most holy place through the sacrifice of Jesus. His sacrifice has opened the way for us to come boldly to the throne of grace.

The Holy Place was where only the priests could enter to do the work of the ministry, a place for tending to the holy things prescribed by God. Rituals were performed to honor God in this sacred room where everything was made of gold. This is representative of our spirits. As kings and priests of God, we live and minister to the Lord in our hearts. Nothing outside of God gets into this part of our heart, and nothing outside of God comes out from it. This part of our heart is holy, having been cleansed by the blood of Jesus. It is born again and sealed.

In the temple's Holy Place, there were three different furnishings, all symbolic of a new creation. To the right, there was the table of showbread, which was also called *the bread of the presence*. It was always to be in God's presence, and it represented God's willingness to fellowship with man as in the breaking of bread at a meal. There was a *golden lampstand* to the left, a reminder that the light of God was always present. There was an *altar of incense ahead*—a symbol of prayer going up to God. God wanted people to know they could approach Him.

The priests ate the old bread after the new was brought in. The twelve "old" loaves represented the foundation of the Old Covenant—the twelve tribes of Israel. The twelve "new" loaves represented the New Covenant, established through the twelve apostles. The sum total of twenty-four are the elders of God's temple represented in Revelation 4. They are the foundation of a building (Jesus said we're the "living stones" with which He will build), and they are symbolic of the work of the church in the earth today. The church is a living temple, Jesus being the chief cornerstone. In our spirits, we are priests unto God, and as we feed on God's Word—the bread of life—we grow stronger each day.

The golden lampstand was tended by the priest and was never to go out, as it was the only source of light. It was called the menorah and was made up of a center candle with three candles on each side, making a total of seven candles. These represent the seven eyes of the Lord, which Isaiah lists as the Spirit of the Lord, wisdom, understanding, counsel, might, knowledge, and the fear of the Lord. Your spirit is born of these eyes that illuminate your heart; your spirit is filled with nothing but light (Isaiah 11:2).

The altar of incense is where the priest burned a sweet-smelling incense every morning and evening. It rose to the ceiling through the opening above the veil and ministered to God in the most holy place (the second chamber). Our born-again spirit is a sweet smelling incense to God for eternity. Our worship in spirit and truth is a blessing to God. In our spirit man, we have been made kings and priests, and we now offer bloodless sacrifices to God in thanksgiving, praise, and worship with all our hearts (1 Peter 2:9).

> *From Jesus Christ, who is the faithful witness, and the first begotten of the dead, and the prince of the kings of the earth. Unto him that loved us, and washed us from our sins in his own blood, and **hath made us kings and priests unto God, and his Father; to him be glory and dominion forever and ever.* Amen.*
>
> Revelation 1:5-6 KJV [Emphasis mine]

> *And hast made us unto our God **kings and priests**: and we shall reign on the earth.*
>
> Revelation 5:10 KJV [Emphasis mine]

The most holy place—behind the veil—was where the shekinah glory of God dwelt. It was a place reserved exclusively for the high priest, who would enter only once a year to make atonement and intercession for the people. It contained the ark of the covenant, which had a mercy seat between two angels on top. The mercy seat, as defined in the Hebrew, represents the *wiping out*, or *the thing of cleansing*.

The ark is another representation of the salvation God provides. On this side of the cross, we have a high priest who has entered the most holy place once and for all. Jesus Christ has removed the veil that once separated us from intimacy with God. He has united us to His Spirit and forever makes intercession for us before the Father.

The veil was torn at the exact moment of Christ's death. It signified how Jesus made a way through the veil of His flesh torn at the cross for us, so we could have a relationship with God once again. Because of the cross, nothing can separate us from our Father.

Our born-again spirit is now intimately connected with Jesus' spirit as one. God's shekinah (dwelling) glory is fully and completely united to our spirits.

> *For in Him dwells all the fullness of the Godhead bodily.*
> Colossians 2:9

> *Though He was a Son, yet He learned obedience by the things which He suffered. And having been perfected, He became the author of eternal salvation to all who obey Him, called by God as High Priest "according to the order of Melchizedek."*
> Hebrews 5:8-10

> *Who being the brightness of His glory and the express image of His person and upholding all things by the word of His power, when He had by Himself purged our sins, sat down at the right hand of the Majesty on high.*
> Hebrews 1:3

Right now, since Christ is in us and we are in Him, we too have access into that holiest of all places where we can stand and commune directly with the manifested presence of God. God's glory is not a cloud filling a room.

His glory is His manifested presence and person, something that affects us supernaturally in our everyday lives. Healing is His glory manifested. Peace in our hearts is His glory manifested. Provision for our daily needs is His glory manifested. The glory of God is the demonstration of all His goodness and the provision of Jesus' sacrifice.

> *So God has given both his promise and his oath. These two things are unchangeable because it is impossible for God to lie. Therefore, we who have fled to him for refuge can have great confidence as we hold to the hope that lies before us.*
>
> *This hope is a strong and trustworthy anchor for our souls. It leads us through the curtain into God's inner sanctuary. Jesus has already gone in there for us. He has become our eternal High Priest in the order of Melchizedek.*
>
> Hebrews 6:18-20 NLT

On this side of the cross—the conquering side—our soul is anchored to our spirit man. Our spirit man is intimately linked to our High Priest Jesus Christ, which gives us access to the power of God and the ability to overcome anything we face in this life.

Before the marvelous work of the cross, God's manifested presence had to be masked with a cloud in order to protect the people from the devastation of His goodness compared to their situation. Because of sin and our fallen state in Adam, we simply could not stand in God's unveiled presence. It was a matter of law.

3|10|2)

Now, Jesus has paid the price under the law, and with sin forever atoned and our new condition in Christ, we can stand and fellowship with our God. We are God's copies of the Master, Jesus. Our eyes should be on the fact that all He is and all He has are now a part of our spirit man.

The shekinah glory that was in the most holy place in Solomon's temple is the same glory that is in our spirit. When you think about it, His glory living in you is no greater a mystery than His glory dwelling in Moses' tabernacle—a tent in the wilderness.

If God was able to sanctify, manifest, and do such marvelous works in those old tabernacles and temples made with man's hands, how much more do you think He has sanctified a part of you—your spirit—as His very own tabernacle?

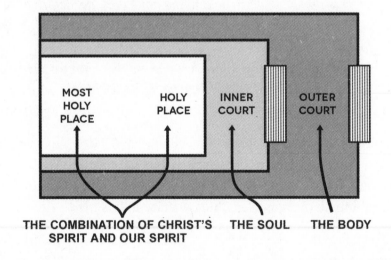

MOST HOLY PLACE   **HOLY PLACE**   **INNER COURT**   **OUTER COURT**

THE COMBINATION OF CHRIST'S SPIRIT AND OUR SPIRIT   **THE SOUL**   **THE BODY**

With the correct picture of who you are now in Christ, it's easy to see the realities of all the other scriptures that declare the goodness of God in our lives. Would God ever desire to put sickness on His own house? Would depression or despair or lack ever be something that God willed for the holiest of all? You are the temple of God!

You are precious in the eyes of the Lord! You are the place where He has chosen to live and shine as a light for the entire world to see and believe. You just have to receive this by faith and be willing to stand on it, believing whole-heartedly in this miraculous work of God in your life.

God has forever joined the two chambers together, and we are now one spirit with the Lord. What God has joined together (Christ and our spirit), let no man put asunder.

> *For we know that when this earthly tent we live in is taken down (that is, when we die and leave this earthly body), we will have a house in heaven, an eternal body made for us by God himself and not by human hands. We grow weary in our present bodies, and we long to put on our heavenly bodies like new clothing. For we will put on heavenly bodies; we will not be spirits without bodies. While we live in these earthly bodies, we groan and sigh, but it's not that we want to die and get rid of these bodies that clothe us. Rather, we want to put on our new bodies so that these dying bodies will be swallowed up by life. God himself has prepared us for this, and as a guarantee he has given us his Holy Spirit. So we are always confident, even though we know that as long as we live in these bodies we are not at home with the Lord. **For we live by believing and not by seeing.**
>
> 2 Corinthians 5:1-7 NLT [Emphasis mine]

None of this is overly complicated, and yet, many people struggle with seeing the reality of these simple pictures come to pass in their lives. It just boils down to living and walking by faith and not by sight. Plain and simple, most people are judging the Word of God by their circumstances instead of judging their circumstances by the Word of God. We are to believe what God has said and patiently believe for circumstances to line up with His Word. His Word is eternal truth. It's forever settled in heaven and in earth, and it will never change.

Circumstances are always subject to change when they're challenged by unwavering faith in the Word. Again, I remind you: Your spirit man has been completely changed, but everything on the outside of you requires faith and patience in order to see the manifested promises of God. I like to use the example of breathing. To live, a person has to breathe. You don't "try" to breathe and then come up with an alternative solution if that doesn't work out. Likewise, living by faith is not something you "try." It's something you **do.** There are no alternatives. There is no plan B when it comes to believing or not believing God. The key is to come to an understanding that the Word of God is absolute and undeniable truth. You must come face to face with the fact that it will never fail. And with unwavering determination, we must live by it.

> *For in it the righteousness of God is revealed from faith to faith; as it is written, "The just shall live by faith."*
>
> Romans 1:17

> *But that no one is justified by the law in the sight of God is evident, for "the just shall live by faith."*
>
> Galatians 3:11

> *Now the just shall live by faith; But if anyone draws back, My soul has no pleasure in him.*
>
> Hebrews 10:38

Always remember that without faith, it's impossible to please God. We can measure everything we think and do against that simple scriptural statement. God has plainly told us that it's imperative to trust Him and His Word. It pleases God when we press beyond the body/soul mindset of the world and go on into the spirit-minded lifestyle of His kingdom. That is the spirit and soul combination, with the two linked together. To be carnally-minded is death, but to be spiritually minded is life and peace. When we're spiritually minded, it pleases God and blesses us.

Faith doesn't come by having heard some scriptures here and there. It only comes as you continually and relentlessly meditate in the Word. This is a search for treasure. You can never stop being renewed in the spirit of your mind. You can never stop studying to show yourself approved unto God, allowing the Word to transform you into the image of His Son. You don't need to be brainwashed, but you certainly do need your brain washed from the filth of this world by the water of the Word. When you renew your mind to the authenticity of the perfect work of Christ in your spirit, your life will be continually transformed. It will prove the good and perfect will of God, and His good desires for you will be demonstrated and put into the daily action of your life.

However, I caution you to be a doer of the Word and not only a hearer. Without personal disciplines that promote the renewing of your mind, you will be conformed to the things of the world and fall prey to the enemy's devices. It's not hard to make a few simple adjustments to your daily routines—making a place for the treasure that can be discovered in His Word and purposing to seek Him. It's guaranteed to change your entire life. The Word reveals and releases new creation realities as your soul agrees. This is the discovery of your new identity in Christ. Once **discovered** your identity also needs to be **recovered.** Having your mind renewed by the Spirit of God's Word begins this recovery process of walking in the light of who you are.

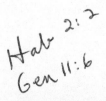
Hab 2:2
Gen 11:6

CHAPTER TWELVE
HEART & SWORD

The heart of man is one of the greatest mysteries in all the universe. It is complex, fascinating, and a wonderful aspect of God's creation. The heart is one of the most important subjects for a Christian to understand, while also being the most difficult to define and explain.

While heart surgeons can understand and even operate on our physical hearts and scientists can define our molecular structure and DNA make-up, man struggles to comprehend our figurative heart. While we can divide the atom and define the base elements of life as we know them, our own heart remains a mystery outside of a revelation of God's Word.

If we are to properly seat our true identity in our hearts, we need to find a way of defining and dividing our hearts.

> *For the **word of God** is living and powerful, and sharper than any two-edged sword, piercing even to the division of **soul and spirit**, and of joints and marrow, and is a discerner of the thoughts and intents of the **heart.***
>
> Hebrews 4:12 [Emphasis mine]

Two powerful truths are revealed in this one passage: The hardest thing in the cosmos to divide is the heart, and the sharpest thing in the universe that can do it is God's Word. In an attempt to explain the power and life of God's Word, let's consider the most difficult things to divide: spirit from soul, joints from marrow, and thoughts from intentions of the heart. God's Word is so sharp it can divide and discern the heart—even in regard to the soul and spirit. That, my friends, is how impressive God's Word is.

The apostle Paul defines the life and power that comes when we allow the Word to define our hearts and, consequently, define our identity. Philosophies fail, fall, and stumble in attempts to explain man's heart. Science, with all its theories and textbooks, again fumbles in the dark with inconclusive results when it tries to do that which only the Word of God can achieve: define and divide man's heart.

The heart is vital to our relationship with God and our understanding of the work of the cross, especially regarding the new creation (our new identity). A careful search of biblical references relating to the heart leads us to hundreds of scriptures; it's just voluminous. We may not search all references out, but there are basics foundational to fully comprehending the God-given ability to walk out our new identity in Christ and how it all works and relates to the heart. *Heart* in Scripture can mean different things depending on the context.

SPIRIT AND SOUL

Sometimes in Scripture, man is defined as a two-part being (inner man, outer man). Other times, man appears as a three-part being (spirit, soul, and body). Sometimes, *heart* in Scripture is speaking of the spirit of man, while other instances see it referring to the soul of man. In still other cases, it refers to the combination of both. Put simply, the heart of man contains the spirit and the soul; the two are entwined. Spirit and soul are addressed separately in order to teach how the heart functions and what we must do to manifest our new identity. It's the context of the particular passage that will determine if heart is a reference to our spirit (the born-again part of our heart) or our soul (the part of the heart that needs renewal.). With the image of Solomon's temple in mind, this combination of spirit and soul making up our heart can be represented as follows:

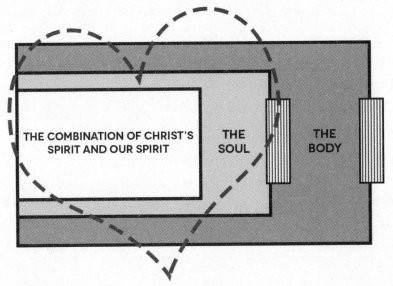

Keep in mind that you are created in the image of a triune God. You are a spiritual being that has a soul, and you live in a body. For simplicity, we refer to man as "spirit, soul, and body." However, though we divide man into three parts, careful study reveals that the spirit and soul of man are deeply intertwined as if you took your hands and weaved together both sets of fingers.

When we refer to the heart, we refer to this meshing of spirit and soul. The earthly body dies, but the soul and spirit are linked and go on living forever.

In Adam, darkness permeated our heart—spirit and soul—and we became dead to the goodness of God. In Christ our spirit is made perfectly new and bright with light. It recognizes our Father's love, and we're made perfectly righteous in His sight. Although we as spiritual beings are saved eternally, our soul needs to catch up. It must wake up to this newness of life. Our soul enters into a process; it is yet "being saved." When the spirit is born again, the soul is still wrapped up with identities from the world and its way of thinking, feeling, and reasoning. This is why the Scripture says we must renew our minds to God's way, which is revealed in His Word.

The soul knows the brightness of the new life that has come, but it still needs to understand what the light means; it needs to be trained not to think in darkness mode anymore.

The following diagram illustrates how the soul can travel and lean either toward the natural realm or the spiritual realm.

The renewed mind of the heart will link us to God's manifestations in life, while the un-renewed mind—even though we are saved eternally—will link us to the world and the manifestations of evil and woe. The soul decides where we abide—in the spiritual or the natural.

The things in the spirit realm can only get into the natural realm through the soul (mind, will, and emotions). It's very important to understand the function of the heart or inner man, because every issue of life stems from it. Your health, wealth, wisdom, understanding, and every personal relationship is completely affected by how your heart responds to the spiritual world—the light or the dark side of things. In very simple terms: The spirit world is like Star Wars in that you have the good guys and the bad guys, the light side and the dark side. And since we are spirits living in bodies, we can choose where we connect. God cautions us to pay close attention to what is in us because whatever is in our hearts will eventually make its way into our lives.

> *Guard your heart above all else, for it determines the course of your life.*
>
> Proverbs 4:23 NLT

The soul has a lot of power. It can choose what will dominate you. The physical body and our emotions are very big to us. We deal with these things every minute of every day, and we often forget that they're subject to the fallen world. The spirit of God in a Christian is different and superior. As a result, there's a war going on—constantly. It's always a two-vs.-one scenario. The soul can join up with the renewed spirit by thinking on God's Word and meditating on it day and night, or the soul can join up with the body by agreeing with what is seen in the natural, following the five senses and philosophies of those in Adam.

Spirit + Soul = Power. The combination of the spirit and soul releases power over the body and our life in the natural world. It allows for a complete victory, one that experiences God's best at every level.

Body + Soul = No power. The combination of the body and soul cancels out power against darkness and oppression. The negatives of this world will override your perfect, righteous, and overcoming spirit.

THE SWORD OF THE SPIRIT

No other scripture in the Word of God draws the complete picture of the heart more clearly than Hebrews 4:12. It shows beyond doubt that there are two distinct ways the heart interprets what comes into it and what goes out.

> *For the word of God is living and powerful, and sharper than any **two-edged sword**, piercing even to the division of **soul and spirit**, and of **joints and marrow**, and is a discerner of the **thoughts and intents** of the **heart.***
>
> Hebrews 4:12 [Emphasis mine]

The heart has an interior battle going on between the spirit (belonging to God) and the un-renewed mind (the soul, which has been trained to follow fallen-world thinking, doing, and feeling). These parts of the heart often seem inseparable, yet the Word of God is able to rightly divide them, giving you the clarity you need to always walk in truth, righteousness, love, and power.

This passage defines the heart as the combination of soul and spirit. It also delineates what is in these two chambers of our heart, as well as how each chamber functions. There's nothing under the sun that can separate the mysterious merging of soul and spirit to reveal the thoughts and intents of the heart. No logical thinking or psychology can pierce deeply enough to divide the soul and spirit. No intellectual consideration can figure out how the soul and spirit function as a unit—man would simply go crazy trying to figure it out. The heart is a supernatural bond of such intricacy that the Lord impresses upon us that only His Sword—sharper than any other two-edged sword—can separate the two.

God's Word and God's Word alone is the only thing that can divide and discern what's coming out of what part of the heart: soul or spirit. It reveals what is of the soul (carnal) and what is of the spirit (of God). Did your most recent thought come from your un-renewed soul or your born-again spirit? God's Word can tell you. Was the voice I heard God's voice—He who is united to my spirit? Or was it just my own imagination coming out of my soul? God's Word can divide and discern.

The following illustration shows how God's word (His divine sword) divides the soul and spirit that make up the heart. Hebrews 4:12 shows what falls under soul and what falls under spirit. Joints fall under the soul and marrow is under the spirit; thoughts are under the soul and intentions are under the spirit.

3/24
Acts 17

GOD'S WORD
SWORD OF THE SPIRIT
HEB. 4:12

SOUL

JOINTS
- Connect things

THOUGHTS
- Mind, will & emotions
- Can be carnal or
  spiritual
- Life comes through it
- Must be renewed

SPIRIT

MARROW
- Produces blood (life)
- Born-Again

INTENTS
- Always knows & is willing
  to do the right thing
- It has the mind of
  Christ
- Is united to Christ
- Life comes from
  the spirit

motives

The soul part of the heart is referred to as having joints and thoughts. In the same way that joints connect different parts of the human body with each other, the soul connects with the spirit and with the flesh. It is the joint between the spirit world and the natural world. As a result, the soul can be spirit-minded or carnal-minded. The spirit side of the heart, however, is described as having marrow and intents. In our bodies, bone marrow produces blood, and blood carries life. The marrow spoken of in Hebrews illustrates that our new identity in Christ, filled with life and power, comes from the spirit side of the heart. However, everything flows through the soul (the joint), thus the need for its renewal. Our intents from the spirit are always correct, true, right, and good, but our thoughts and feelings need to be renewed for those intents to be experienced. That renewal is brought about through the Word of God.

The Word is called "the sword of the spirit" because, as a blade, it divides the soul from the spirit. It lets the contents of man's thinking and feeling be clearly seen—whether it be of God's life (the reborn spirit) or of the natural (the old habits of the soul thinking like the fallen world).

The Word divides between our identity with newness of life and our identity with an old life in bondage. It reveals the condition of our heart as a whole—are we in glory territory or the no-longer-valid "swampy ground"? One is health in all aspects of life, while the other is the land of sin, sickness, and disease. So, we are admonished:

> *My son give attention to my words; Incline your ear to my sayings. Do not let them depart from your eyes; Keep them in the midst of your heart; For they are life to those who find them, And health to all their flesh. Keep your heart with all diligence, for out of it spring the issues of life.*
>
> Proverbs 4:20-23

The word keep in the original Hebrew language literally means to guard. We're to guard or protect our heart with all diligence, attentiveness, and persistence, so we'll reap a bountiful harvest of God's blessings.

> *So He said to them, "Are you thus without understanding also? Do you not perceive that whatever enters a man from outside cannot defile him, because it does not enter his heart but his stomach, and is eliminated, thus purifying all foods?" And He said, "What comes out of a man, that defiles a man. For from within, out of the heart of men, proceed evil thoughts, adulteries, fornications, murders, thefts,*

covetousness, wickedness, deceit, lewdness, an evil eye, blasphemy, pride, foolishness. All these evil things come from within and defile a man."

Mark 7:18-23

When Jesus spoke of evil things coming out of our hearts, He was speaking of the soul side of our hearts and not the spirit side. Things can get into and come out of the soul part of our heart, but not the spirit part. That's why, even after salvation, we must be vigilant to guard the heart (soul).

CIRCUMCISION OF THE HEART

In the Old Testament, when a male Hebrew child was born, he was circumcised to give him the mark of the covenant—the imprint or label of God. It was not a label that said "Ralph Lauren" or "Taco Bell" or "Presbyterian" or "Catholic" or any other name, but a label that said "My people." Circumcision permanently declared a man's position as a Jew, a member of the family of God. It's awkward to speak of, but it's a profound symbol that this mark was made by a blade and given in the place where the seed of man emanates. It's given where the seed would spring forth to perpetuate God's people in a special relationship with God, rooted in covenant. It was a daily reminder for a man and a wife, a reminder of the covenant they had with each other and with the one true God. But still, God always spoke of the heart. He was always after the heart because this was His original plan and design for man.

So, circumcise [that is, remove sin from] your heart, and be stiff-necked (stubborn, obstinate) no longer.

Deuteronomy 10:16 AMP

Notice God was pointing to circumcision of the heart. An uncircumcised heart would always be stubborn, obstinate, prideful, and resistant to God.

> *And the Lord your God will circumcise your heart and the heart of your descendants, to love the Lord your God with all your heart and with all your soul, that you may live.*
>
> Deuteronomy 30:6

This is a promise that God would eventually change man's heart so our love for God would come from a pure heart. Notice again that after the circumcision of our hearts, we would (not just could, but would) love God with all (not just part) of our heart and soul.

In the New Testament after the cross, Paul made it clear that our heart is the central issue:

> *For you are not a true Jew just because you were born of Jewish parents or because you have gone through the ceremony of circumcision. No, a true Jew is **one whose heart is right** with God. And true circumcision is not merely obeying the letter of the law; rather, it is a **change of heart** produced by the Spirit. And a person with a **changed heart** seeks praise from God, not from people.*
>
> Romans 2:28-29 NLT [Emphasis mine]

WITH ALL YOUR HEART

The most important commandment is loving God with all your heart.

> *Jesus replied, "The most important commandment is this: 'Listen, O Israel! The Lord our God is the one and only Lord.*

*And you must love the Lord your God with **all your heart**, all your soul, all your mind, and all your strength.'"*

Mark 12:29-30 NLT [Emphasis mine]

This is not an ordinary "Yeah, I love ice cream" thing or an "I go to church every Sunday" thing. It's every day, whole heart, all out. It's commanded to love Him with all our soul (the seat of emotions), all our mind (thoughts, will, intellect), and all our strength. Notice all these different aspects of our being: Our heart, our soul, our mind, and our strength. This speaks of every part of our earthly life. Loving God with all our heart is the opposite of loving Him with a divided heart. A divided heart has one part in God's kingdom and another in the world. A divided heart is not just a "lukewarm heart" or what some might call an "all-inclusive" heart or a "tolerant of everyone" heart. The scripture calls it a "hard" heart. This is because you cannot serve two masters.

No one can serve two masters. For you will hate one and love the other; you will be devoted to one and despise the other.

Matthew 6:24 NLT

More evidence we DON'T lose salvation, but are not completely committed in body: soul.

When we don't love God with our whole soul (with emotions under His control instead of emotions under the control of our circumstances), we become prey to our enemies—fear, doubt, and worry. We must sell out to God with every aspect of our being or our entire existence will be adversely affected.

Deuteronomy 28 says:

Because you did not serve the Lord your God with a heart full of joy and gladness for the abundance of all things [with which He blessed you], you will therefore serve your enemies.... (feM, depression, etc)

Deuteronomy 28:47-48 AMP

Isaiah the prophet speaks of loving God with our mind, and through this love, we can think and reason with God (Isaiah 1:18). The Bible does not say we're transformed by the removal of our mind but rather by the renewal of it. So, we can think of one part of our relationship with God as being in school and having a frank discussion with our professor—a good, sit-down talk about what's going on, what we don't understand, and what we don't like. It's okay to reason with God. It's just not okay to reason against God.

God's divine design has always been to deal with the inner man and direct him in the affairs of life from the heart. God created Adam from the dust of the earth and breathed into him the breath of life, at which point he became a "living soul" (Genesis 2:7). God's Spirit was united to Adam's, bringing life to his soul and body. Adam served and fellowshipped with God through a heart filled with God's Spirit. He loved God with all his heart, soul, mind, and body.

A NEW HEART

When Adam fell, the spirit that was in him departed, leaving him spiritually vacant. It wasn't that his spirit ceased to exist, but that his spirit ceased to exist in union with the Spirit of God. God did not leave him or forsake him, and God did not "cut him off" from blessings because He was angry. On the contrary, God loved Adam and moved to protect him from remaining in a bad state. He put him out of the garden—away from the tree of life—to prevent him from eating of it and thereby living forever in a fallen condition. He set a course for restoration, and He continued to fellowship with Adam. However, it was a very different kind of fellowship. God still loved

Adam the same as He always had, but Adam's love for God had changed. It was clouded. It had become distant and confused. He lost his trust in God.

Adam experienced a "negative rebirth." He went from having a spirit full of the life of God to having a spirit full of the prince of the power of the air. He entered the opposing life of Satan. The New Testament declares that man, in his fallen condition in Adam, unconsciously walked under the influence of the "prince of the power of the air" (Ephesians 2:2), which refers to the fallen spirit world where Satan wields his own kind of power of deception.

The scripture refers to it as darkness. On the "dark side," the warmth of God's light is gone. And where there is no light, things become cold. Therefore, the Word says that man's heart became cold or as a stone. It became hardened—no longer sensitive to God's voice, no longer sensitive to God's ways, and no longer engaged in the attributes of God, such as justice, mercy, and faith. **This is why God sent Jesus to rescue man, to bring him back into the light.** This is why Jesus is called "the light of the world."

In Him was life, and the life was the light of men.

John 1:4

At the fall, God's proximity with man was altered. God went from being inside of a man's heart to being on the outside of his heart. With few exceptions, it stayed that way until the cross. But all along—from the fall to the cross—God spoke through His prophets about the work He would do by Jesus. He would again take up residence in man's heart. With a new heart, a new soul, and a renewed mind—all under the influence of God's life-giving power— man would gravitate toward the light and be affected for good in all his being and doing.

And I will give them one heart [a new heart], and put a new spirit within them. I will take from them the heart of stone, and will give them a heart of flesh [that is responsive to My touch].

Ezekiel 11:19 AMP

This is what God does at the new birth. The minute we accept Christ as Lord, God changes our heart. Our heart is a part of us that contains both the soul (the mind, will, emotions) and the spirit (the breath of life). God changes the part of our heart that has our spirit in it. He tangibly changes our spirit. From the new spirit, He can change the rest of our heart—the soul, the mind, will, and emotions.

*But this shall be the covenant that I will make with the house of Israel; After those days, saith the LORD, I will put my law in their inward parts, **and write it in their hearts**; and will be their God, and they shall be my people.*

Jeremiah 31:33 KJV [Emphasis mine]

God declared He would literally remove the stony heart of fallen man and miraculously replace it with a pliable heart, and He would permanently seal it by the power of His Holy Spirit. A sealed heart is one given to God by free will, by a conscious, deliberate choice. It cannot be stolen; it is sealed with a Holy Spirit "God mark." In the old days, a king would seal a letter with melted wax and press that wax with the imprint of his signet ring to prove that the message was truly from the king. This prevented anyone from tampering with it. God sends His message via Jesus! Every time it's received, it bears the imprint of His Spirit—as though he has stamped His signet ring on the soft wax of our heart.

For all of this to occur, man had to realize he was living in a poor condition; in effect, he lived in spiritual poverty. He had to understand he was lost. More than that, man had to realize he could not get out of that condition on his own. He would have to have a reference point to find his way. This is why God instituted the law—to show the impossibility of attaining a right mind and a right life by our own effort, our own works. Man alone could never live up to the standard of righteousness; for all his striving, he could never fulfill the law. Before the cross, God spoke in outward, law-abiding terms, always working in an effort to reach man's heart. The law was intended to demonstrate man's weakness and bring awareness to say, "You need help. You need a savior." It worked to reveal how hopeless and helpless we are without God.

> *Therefore the law was our tutor to bring us to Christ, that we might be justified by faith.*
>
> Galatians 3:24

> *Therefore by the deeds of the law there shall no flesh be justified in his sight; for by the law is the knowledge of sin.*
>
> Romans 3:20 KJV

The law was created to make sin known. How is that good? It's good in its ability to drive us toward God, causing us to depend on His goodness rather than our own corrupt hearts and their darkened, distorted world view. Our inability to keep the law reveals our weakness, pushing and driving us toward God's strength. Our un-holiness revealed shows us our need for God's holiness.

Notice again in Romans 3:20 that the law was given to reveal sin, not God. Moses (law) was given to reveal our sin and weakness. Jesus (grace) came to reveal God and His glory. Moses shows us what is wrong, while Jesus through our simple faith makes us right. At the cross, Jesus substituted Himself for us. He took our inadequacy and gave us His goodness and strength in exchange. He changed us and gave us the ability to love Him with all of our heart. Accepting Jesus creates a mysterious, supernatural change inside of us. God's Spirit returns to take up a new residence within us, so He can speak directly to us in our heart.

> *The spirit of a man is the lamp of the Lord, searching all the inner depths of his heart.*
>
> Proverbs 20:27

It will take some meditation to allow these truths to penetrate your life. God cares about everything concerning you, and Jesus has redeemed every single part of your life. Although the power of this Christian life doesn't come from the soul, it does come through the soul. That's why we must renew our minds to God's truth about us. As a Christian, there's only one place to be—God's Word.

The key to the Christian life is in renewing our mind to what God has done in our spirit at the new birth. He changed our identity! Once our mind is renewed, our "God-heart" life can begin to flow freely into the natural realm unabated, producing goodness, health, wealth, joy, transformation, and all the fruit of the Spirit.

CHAPTER THIRTEEN
TRANSFORMATION

Being forgiven and missing out on the devil's hell is a lot, but that is not what the new birth is all about. Jesus didn't go to the cross just to get you to heaven; He went to the cross to bring heaven to you now.

> *And by Him to reconcile all things to Himself, by Him, whether things on earth or things in heaven, having made peace through the blood of His cross. And you, who once were alienated and enemies in your mind by wicked works, yet now He has reconciled in the body of His flesh through death, to present you holy, and blameless, and above reproach in His sight.*
>
> Colossians 1:20-22

Everything Jesus did was about reconciliation and restoration. He gave His life as a ransom to buy you back, to bring you into a close, personal, one-on-one relationship with Him where the powers of darkness can no longer manipulate and control you because you're in Christ. Because of the cross, we've been relocated into God's kingdom, out of Satan's reach.

I pray you will see this is a spiritual condition, not a physical one.

> *For this reason we also, since the day we heard it, do not cease to pray for you, and to ask that you may be filled with the knowledge of His will in all wisdom and spiritual understanding; that you may walk worthy of the Lord, fully pleasing Him, being fruitful in every good work and increasing in the knowledge of God; strengthened with all might, according to His glorious power, for all patience and longsuffering with joy; giving thanks to the Father who has qualified us to be partakers of the inheritance of the saints in the light. He has delivered us from the power of darkness and conveyed us into the kingdom of the Son of His love.*
>
> Colossians 1:9-13

Much like a criminal who truly "comes clean"—leaves behind a life of crime, testifies against his fellow crooks, and enters a witness protection program—we can never go back to our former life. When someone turns from a life of crime, the witness protection program offers him a new life with a brand-new start. The protected individual is given a new name, a new look, and a new home someplace far away. The person's new identity will keep him safe from the enemies who desire to destroy him.

> *But God demonstrates His own love toward us, in that while we were still sinners, Christ died for us. Much more then, having now been justified by His blood, we shall be saved from wrath through Him. For if when we were enemies we were **reconciled to God** through the death of His Son, much more, having been reconciled, we shall be saved by His life.*
>
> Romans 5:8-10 [Emphasis mine]

And you hath he quickened [made alive], *who were dead in trespasses and sins; Wherein* **in time past** *ye walked according to the course of this world, according to the prince of the power of the air, the spirit that now worketh in the children of disobedience: Among whom also we all had our conversation [life]* **in times past** *in the lusts of our flesh, fulfilling the desires of the flesh and of the mind; and were by nature the children of wrath, even as others.*

Ephesians 2:1-3 KJV [Emphasis and brackets mine]

Before any Christian was saved, we were kingdom "criminals" by nature and associated with other kingdom criminals in the group of fallen man. Whether we realized it or not, we were enemies of God—children of wrath who followed the fallen prince Satan. We were all gang members who decided to get out of the gang, change our way of life, and live unto God. And wouldn't you know it, those same people we ran with in the world are now the ones who rail against us and the new life we've chosen.

For we have spent enough **of our past lifetime** *in doing the will of the Gentiles—when we walked in lewdness, lusts, drunkenness, revelries, drinking parties, and abominable idolatries. In regard to these, they think it strange that you do not run with them in the same flood of dissipation, speaking evil of you. They will give an account to Him who is ready to judge the living and the dead.*

1 Peter 4:3-5 [Emphasis mine]

When you're born again, you enter God's witness protection program. He gives you a new life, and a new kingdom to live in. He gives you a new name—Jesus, which is above every name. He gives you new clothes—robes of righteousness. He gives you His own armor, which is impenetrable. He gives you a new identity with the King of kings and Lord of lords.

You may not **feel** like anything has changed, but in your spirit **everything** has changed. The old man has died, and there's a new man in you. Christ is in you! He says, "You are now created in righteousness, and I am giving you a brand-new start, a brand-new life—everlasting life!"

> *For God so loved the world that He gave His only begotten Son, that whoever believes in Him should not perish but have everlasting life.*
>
> John 3:16

> *And this is eternal life, that they may know You, the only true God, and Jesus Christ whom You have sent.*
>
> John 17:3

In God's witness protection program, you get a "new look" that is full of the fruit of the Spirit. You learn to put on the new man, one who is selfless, God-centered, and other-people-minded. You are radically separated from the world. You are given kingdom authority through the name of Jesus to exercise the power of God as His personal ambassador. And as if all that was not enough, you've been freed from the powers of darkness.

> *Grace to you and peace from God the Father and our Lord Jesus Christ, who gave Himself for our sins, that He might **deliver us from this present evil age**, according to the will of our God and Father, to whom be glory forever and ever. Amen.*
>
> Galatians 1:3-5 [Emphasis mine]

Not only are you a resident of this new kingdom, but as we've seen, you've been made a king and a priest, ruling and reigning with Jesus. You don't even have to understand it at first. The fact of the matter is, you have a new ID, so you need to kick the devil in the teeth and live in it. This is obedience in accordance with God's Word.

Before salvation, you were only a resident of this present, earthly habitation, bound by the limitations of natural life and controlled primarily by negative powers. You probably didn't even know that's who you were. Yet, in your new life, you're still in this world, but you're not of this world. You are a supernatural man or woman, seated in heavenly places in Christ Jesus, and God has given you the guarantee of His Spirit, a confirmation of all He's promised.

> *Who also has sealed us and given us the Spirit in our hearts as a guarantee.*
>
> 2 Corinthians 1:22

We've been empowered with the very power of God.

> *Now to Him who is able to do exceedingly abundantly above all that we ask or think, according to **the power that works in us**, to Him be glory in the church by Christ Jesus to all generations, forever and ever. Amen.*
>
> Ephesians 3:20-21 [Emphasis mine]

Notice, God is able to do for us now according to the power at work in us.

THE NEW YOU

When you learn to walk according to this new life that's in you, you can overcome any obstacle. You just need to know you've been placed in God's witness protection program, and you must let go of your past self (the old man in Adam). You absolutely have to let go of your old life. You're not a criminal hanging out with other criminals anymore. Granted, for many people, *criminal* is probably a strong word. So look at it this way: Maybe you are a "good person" (in your own way of thinking), but that's still far short of what is good and perfect. It's also short of who your Father is and what He wants for you. You are outside of what God has for you when you do not allow your new identity to take charge of your life. This new life is phenomenal! You are a saint with all the rights and privileges of a marvelous, powerful kingdom. You have the righteousness of God dwelling within, right here, right now.

Your old man is dead. Can you get that? Dead! Your old condition in Adam is dead! Embrace your new condition, your new spirit and live in your new kingdom with your new family.

> *This I say, therefore, and testify in the Lord, that you should no longer walk as the rest of the Gentiles walk, in the futility of their mind, having their understanding darkened, being alienated from the life of God, because of the ignorance that is in them, because of the **blindness** of their heart; who, being past feeling, have given themselves over to lewdness, to work all uncleanness with greediness.*
>
> Ephesians 4:17-19 [Emphasis mine]

The Gentiles that Paul was referring to were the non-Christian people who lived among them, the people who were not in covenant with God. These Gentiles lived in a way that was contrary to God, so Paul admonished the new Christians to no longer live that lifestyle.

Essentially, he was saying, "You belong to the Lord, so don't act like the others in the world. Don't just give in to your lusts. The god of this world has blinded their minds, but you're no longer blind."

The Holy Spirit is sealed in your heart, and He can guide you into all truth, separating you from things that hinder. Check your heart! You can see the truth of all things if you will attend to it. You have the eyes of God, so use them!

> *And I will ask the Father, and he will give you another Advocate, who will never leave you. He is the Holy Spirit, who leads into all truth. The world cannot receive him, because it isn't looking for him and doesn't recognize him. But you know him, because he **lives with you** now and later **will be in you.***
>
> John 14:16-17 NLT [Emphasis mine]

Most people in the world are ignorant of spiritual forces. I'm no exception. I was definitely ignorant and alienated from God before I was connected with the incredible love of Christ. So, people are bound by their perceptions. But as Christians, our heart is no longer bound, so we need to quit acting and talking like Gentiles (those in Adam). Paul did not write to the Gentiles that they should quit acting like Gentiles. The Gentiles couldn't help acting like they did—they were Gentiles! Their behavior was just an outflow of who they were: people separated from God. That's why it is a waste of time to condemn the lost for their sin. A sinner sins, just like a dog barks. A person cannot quit sinning until they get out of Adam and into Christ. That would be like a dog deciding he's going to moo like a cow instead of barking like the dog he is. In Adam, sins are just the out-working of a sinful condition.

Now, if all this is true—and it is—then holiness is the byproduct of our new identity in Christ. We need to act like who we are—saints renewed in their minds doing good and mighty works as a result. As you're renewed to the amazing reality of who you are now, your actions will begin to reflect your new condition, which is the result of a good tree that brings forth good fruit.

> *But now you are free from the power of sin and have become slaves [servants] of God. Now you do those things that lead to holiness and result in eternal life.*
>
> Romans 6:22 NLT [Brackets mine]

Holiness is a fruit, so therefore, if the root is holy, then the fruit will be holy. Jesus, who lives in you, is that root:

> *And there shall come forth a rod out of the stem of Jesse, and a Branch shall grow out of his roots: And the spirit of the LORD shall rest upon him, the spirit of wisdom and understanding, the spirit of counsel and might, the spirit of knowledge and of the fear of the LORD.*
>
> Isaiah 11:1-2 KJV

> *And since Abraham and the other patriarchs were holy, their descendants will also be holy—just as the entire batch of dough is holy because the portion given as an offering is holy. For if the roots of the tree are holy, the branches will be, too.*
>
> Romans 11:16 NLT

> *And again, Isaiah says: "There shall be a root of Jesse; And He who shall rise to reign over the Gentiles, In Him the Gentiles shall hope."*
>
> Romans 15:12

PUT ON THE *NEW* MAN

4/21/21

The word *repent* means to *change your mind and direction,* and I assure you that your direction will not change until your mind

Acts 2¹

changes. Many believers stubbornly refuse to let go of their old ideas. This keeps them locked in a world of hardship that God does not will for them. It's hopeless to try and put on the new if you keep thinking like the old. This is why it's so important we read and study the Scriptures, pray the Word of God, and continually seek the Lord for understanding. We must ardently expect insight and believe for the eyes of our understanding to be enlightened.

It's also imperative we get connected to a spiritual father or mother who can mentor us, showing us how to grasp our position, value, and power in Christ. Fathers and mothers help us to mature into the believers God has called us to be. When I say fathers and mothers, I'm simply referring to seasoned and matured believers in the faith, those who have experience in applying God's Word to their lives, situations, and circumstances.

> *But you have not so learned Christ, if indeed you have heard Him and have been taught by Him, as the truth is in Jesus: that you put off, concerning your former conduct, the old man which grows corrupt according to the deceitful lusts, and be renewed in the spirit of your mind, and that you put on the new man which was created according to God, in true righteousness and holiness.*
>
> Ephesians 4:20-24

> *And be continually renewed in the spirit of your mind [having a fresh, untarnished mental and spiritual attitude].*
>
> Ephesians 4:23 AMP

Here in Ephesians, Paul calls our mental disposition "the spirit of your mind." This refers to our mental and spiritual viewpoint. I meet a lot of Christians who have what I call "a classic teenage perspective." When I try to help them through some difficulty, they cop an attitude, refusing to take responsibility for their own thinking. There's always an excuse for why things are the way they are in their lives, and it's never their fault. It's always about what happened to them or what somebody did to them, as opposed to their way of thinking about those events. I know we can be injured by others, but to give all the blame to others is to give them the power to hurt you. That's a shame because it's a blessing to be the only one responsible for your attitude.

Your attitude is one of the few things you have control over. You can't do anything about someone's ill intent, hurtful behavior, or selfishness, but you can choose to meditate on the promises of God. Like Paul, you can think yourself happy even in the worst situations. When you learn to do this, other people and the darkened spirit of the world cannot impose their opinions on you. The Word commands us to change our mental disposition so we can be free from the traps and limitations of the world.

In Psalm 119:165, King David says, "Great peace have those who love Your law, and nothing causes them to stumble." Earlier in that Psalm, David also says God's Word is hidden in our heart so we may not sin against Him. God's Word in our hearts empowers us against sin—Wow! How cool is that?

> *I have been crucified with Christ; it is no longer I who live, but Christ lives in me; and the life which I now live in the flesh I live by faith in the Son of God, who loved me and gave Himself for me.*

> Galatians 2:20

If you're going to be a mature disciple of Jesus, you have to wake up! You're very much alive, but it's now the life of Christ in you that should dictate your every move. This can only happen when you put on the new man.

There's no way you can put on the new man if you don't know you have one or, to a greater extent, what he looks like. Right here, I'm jumping up and down with excitement. I'm yelling, "Your new man looks like Jesus!" God had a dream and a purpose for you before you were born. He knew you in your mother's womb, and He hasn't changed His mind. God says, "Put the old man off and the new man on—the one who is restored in my image." The only thing—the only thing!—standing between the old and new in your life is your mind. God's part—sealing His Spirit on the inside of you—is done. Now, as a co-laborer with God, your job is to make everything in your head come in line with the Word of God.

> I beseech you therefore, brethren, by the mercies of God, that ye present your bodies a living sacrifice, holy, acceptable unto God, which is your reasonable service. And be not **conformed** to this world: but be ye **transformed** by the renewing of your mind, that ye may prove what is that good, and acceptable, and perfect, will of God.
>
> Romans 12:1-2 KJV [Emphasis mine]

Because we are now one spirit with the Lord, we have the authority and control over what the body does. Don't allow your body and the appetites of the flesh to rule over you anymore. You are in control of your body.

> Don't you realize that you become the slave of whatever you choose to obey? You can be a slave to sin, which leads to death, or you can choose to obey God, which leads to righteous living. Thank God! Once you were slaves of sin, but now you wholeheartedly obey this teaching we have given

*you. Now you are **free from your slavery to sin**, and you have become **slaves to righteous living.***

Romans 6:16-18 NLT [Emphasis mine]

Understand, however, that renewing your mind to the Word is not the removing of your mind; it is not being empty-headed. Thinking is good; God gave us brains to use. We just need to line everything up with God instead of the god of this world. Then, we will find ourselves increasingly transformed into the full stature of Christ. The Christian life is all about being transformed even though we live in a fallen world.

*My little children, for whom I labor in birth again until Christ is **formed in you**....*

Galatians 4:19 [Emphasis mine]

Spiritual formation is God's plan and purpose for our lives. The transformation that occurs through the renewing of our minds is a likeness to Christ. We're going from an immature state to a mature state in Jesus.

Conformed means to be shaped like, or fashioned alike. Paul is writing to born-again, Spirit-filled believers, encouraging them to not be like the world. Worldliness has to do with the way we think, not the clothes we wear or style of our hair. We need to change our thinking, not necessarily our wardrobe.

METAMORPHOSIS

The Greek origin of the word *transformed* in this context is the word *metamorphoo* (Greek Strong's Number: 3339). *Morphoo* means to *transform* (literal or figurative *metamorphose*), *change,* or *transfigure.*

4/28/21

"Identity" - ch 13 pg 162

Acts - ch 22

Our English word *metamorphosis* comes from this root word. According to the Collins English Dictionary, some definitions of this word are:

1. The action or process of changing in form, shape, or substance; esp. **transformation by supernatural means.**

2. A complete change in the appearance, circumstances, condition, or character of a person, a state of affairs, etc.

3. Change of form in an animal (or plant), or its parts, during post-embryonic development; spec. the process of transformation from an immature form to a different adult form that many insects and other invertebrates, and some vertebrates (e.g., frogs), undergo in the course of maturing.

In Oklahoma talk, metamorphosis is a fuzzy worm turning into a butterfly or a tadpole turning into a bullfrog. These two events in nature are both radical and supernatural. I was taught early on that the worm turning into a butterfly was a type or picture of the new birth. This was only one of many things I was taught that turned out to be very wrong.

Even in the natural definition of the word *metamorphosis*, it clearly states that not only is it a supernatural change, but it is also the process of transformation from an immature form to an adult form. This is **not** what happens when we're born again. Rather, this is what happens when we renew our minds to what has happened in our spirit. The new birth is instantaneous! It happens in the very moment a person confesses Jesus as Lord, and the newness is complete and lacking nothing. Paul wrote that the Greek word *metamorphoo (transformed)* was speaking specifically about mind renewal, not about being born again.

Think about the process of changing from a fuzzy worm to a butterfly. The worm is restricted by gravity, limited in freedom and mobility, and easy prey for other creatures who want to devour it. But after the cocoon experience, the worm finds power over gravity and a newfound freedom that allows it to escape predators. To top it off, the ugly worm is transformed into an amazing beauty. Think about this. Where did the worm get its wings? They were on the inside of him. The whole butterfly was on the inside, but the worm did not put it into practice. He did not demonstrate what was in him until he went into the cocoon and became transformed.

Everything the worm needed was there and available, yet it could not manifest until it went through this radical, supernatural change called metamorphosis.

I must point out again that the apostle Paul clearly taught that you are separate from your body:

> *I beseech you therefore, brethren, by the mercies of God, that **you** present **your bodies** a living sacrifice, holy, acceptable to God, which is your reasonable service.*
>
> Romans 12:1 [Emphasis mine]

This is important to see! You and your body are separate because it's the spirit of life inside you that will allow you to fly high above the sin and death around you.

> *There is therefore now no condemnation to those who are in Christ Jesus, who do not walk according to the flesh, but according to the Spirit. For **the law of the Spirit of life in Christ Jesus has made me free from the law of sin and death.***
>
> Romans 8:1-2 [Emphasis mine]

From the inside out, you are to be transformed into the image of Christ that's already inside of you—Christ in you, the hope of glory. The life of Christ in our spirit is being released in our daily lives as we have our minds renewed to that new life. As we align our thinking with God's, we're conformed into Christ's image. If we continue to think according to this fallen world, we're being conformed, shaped, and molded into the image of that fallen world in Adam.

The tadpole is much the same as the butterfly in regard to metamorphosis. Before the radical change, it's restricted to the underwater world. In this state, it's small, less mobile, and a sure prey. After its transformation, it develops lungs, legs, and a croaker that can make it phenomenally adept in both worlds—water and air. Just like we are in the world but not of the world, we too have been given all we need to exist in two distinct environments, and we are able to thrive in both. Again, everything the tadpole needs to experience the atmospheric world is on the inside of him, yet he cannot prove it until he goes through metamorphosis.

Everything you and I need to succeed in this life is within us in Christ. But without this radical, supernatural change in our lives, we're relegated to the natural and will not experience the grandeur of God's kingdom here on earth. However, through the metamorphosis that takes place as we're renewed in our minds, we will prove the grandeur of God's residence in us.

> *Oh, my dear children! I feel as if I'm going through labor pains for you again, and they will continue until Christ is fully developed in your lives. I wish I were with you right now so I could change my tone. But at this distance I don't know how else to help you.*

> Galatians 4:19-20 NLT

That's an extraordinary statement. The apostle Paul was talking to a company of people who had already accepted Christ in their hearts but had not matured into disciples of Jesus. He said this happened to them because Christ had not yet been formed in them. The Galatians were fully redeemed, but they listened to the voices of the world and the false doctrines of man's religion instead of staying rooted in the Word. Because of this, they were relegated to bondage and the fullness of Christ inside of them was not able to manifest in their lives. Essentially, Paul said, "I know you guys are bullfrogs on the inside, but it's time for you and all the world to see it. So, let's get with the program. It's time to go from being converts (believers) to disciples (mature believers) who think like God."

> *Seek the Lord while He may be found, Call upon Him while He is near. Let the wicked forsake his way, And the unrighteous man **his thoughts;** Let him return to the Lord, And He will have mercy on him; And to our God, For He will abundantly pardon. For My thoughts are not your thoughts, Nor are your ways My ways," says the Lord. For as the heavens are higher than the earth, So are My ways higher than your ways, And My thoughts than your thoughts.*
>
> Isaiah 55:6-9 [Emphasis mine]

Many people interpret this passage to mean that we can never know the thoughts of God. That is not so. We have the mind of Christ and the Spirit of the Lord to lead and guide us into all truth. The Lord is saying here that we need our minds reconfigured to coincide with His higher thoughts. That's really the simple fact in a nutshell. When we allow God's thoughts to completely and relentlessly dominate our soul, an amazing and powerful grace comes to us.

> *Beloved, I pray that you may prosper in all things and be in health, just as your* **soul prospers.**
>
> 3 John 1:2 [Emphasis mine]

A prospering soul is what facilitates what we're in the spirit to manifest in our daily, physical life. As we yield our souls to the truth of God's Word with the Holy Spirit bearing witness, our lives are radically and supernaturally changed for the glory of God in the earth. As believers, we're to forsake not only the wicked ways of our past but also our worldly thoughts that went along with them. That means we have to think about ourselves as God thinks about us. God's prosperity begins and ends with the prosperity of our minds. While the power of the Christian life does not come **from** the soul, it does and has to come **through** the soul. Our will and mind must come into agreement with the perfect, complete work God has done in our spirit.

With our minds renewed to kingdom principles, God's love and true nature releases these new creation realities into our natural world. I meet many people willing to forsake wicked ways but few willing to forsake worldly thoughts. This is why so many believers today are locked into immaturity. I, for one, refuse to remain a fuzzy worm bound by those limitations. I will not be a tadpole restricted to the aquatic world. I'm going to fly like a butterfly and jump like a frog in Christ.

> *If then you were raised with Christ, seek those things which are above, where Christ is, sitting at the right hand of God.* ***Set your mind on things above,*** *not on things on the earth. For you died, and your life is hidden with Christ in God. When Christ who is our life appears, then you also will appear with Him in glory.*
>
> Colossians 3:1-4 [Emphasis mine]

Be anxious for nothing, but in everything by prayer and supplication, with thanksgiving, let your requests be made known to God; and the peace of God, which surpasses all understanding, will guard your hearts and minds through Christ Jesus. Finally, brethren, whatever things are true, whatever things are noble, whatever things are just, whatever things are pure, whatever things are lovely, whatever things are of good report, if there is any virtue and if there is anything praiseworthy—meditate on these things.

Philippians 4:6-8

You will keep him in perfect peace, whose mind is stayed on You, because he trusts in You.

Isaiah 26:3

Trusting God involves the soul. We can't say we're trusting in God in any given situation when we're not harnessing our thoughts and emotions. Spiritual formation and the will of God in transformation involves our thoughts.

This is a major part of our recovery process and the exciting adventure of being conformed into the image of God's dear Son.

For whom He foreknew, He also predestined to be conformed to the image of His Son, that He might be the firstborn among many brethren.

Romans 8:29

CHAPTER FOURTEEN
WE BE TEA

When Jesus prayed for all believers, He said:

> *I do not pray for these alone, but also for those who will believe in Me through their word; that they all may be one, as You, Father, are in Me, and I in You; that they also may be one in Us, that the world may believe that You sent Me. And the glory which You gave Me I have given them, that they may be one just as We are one: **I in them,** and You in Me; that they may be made perfect in one, and that the world may know that You have sent Me, and have **loved them as You have loved Me.***

John 17:20-23 [Emphasis mine]

We ought to read that scripture out loud to ourselves every day. When I read it, I feel the love of God washing over me. I am astounded! It is mind-boggling that He is in Me and I am in Him. He loves us with the same love He has for Jesus.

Many years ago, the Lord gave me an illustration that is simply profound. While I'm always looking for fresh ways to communicate the kingdom, I've not yet found a better illustration for the new creation than the making of tea. Surely, you have either made tea or watched someone else make it. The process requires only three items: a teabag, water, and a container. When you put the teabag and the water into the container, there's a wondrous infusion that takes place. The water gets all into the teabag, and the tea inside the teabag gets all into the water, radically changing the water. When the process is complete, even after you pull the teabag out of the water and throw it into the trash, what do you call the water? *TEA!*

Think about this for a minute. The tea, the leafy substance in the bag, is physically in the trash, yet you now call the water *tea*. If the tea is still the tea, and the water is still the water, why would you call the water *tea*? You call it *tea* because there was such a powerful transformation when the water became permeated with the tea leaves that the two literally became one inside the vessel. This is a beautiful, uncomplicated picture of what happens when the Lord comes to dwell in us. Our spirits dwell within our clay bodies. This makes the "teacup," with our physical body being the outer shell of the cup. Our spirit man is the water inside the cup. Jesus is the "Teabag" that comes to dwell within our spirit, and thus, we are made "tea." As new creations—as tea—we (Jesus and I, Jesus and you) dwell in an inseparable union in an earthen body.

> *We now have this light shining in our hearts, but we ourselves are like **fragile clay jars** containing this great treasure. This makes it clear that our great power is from God, not from ourselves.*
>
> 2 Corinthians 4:7 NLT [Emphasis mine]

When making a cup of tea, we don't look at the substance in the cup and wonder, Which is it? Is it tea, or is it water? We're not confused about it. God is not confused either. There is a "Teabag"

(Jesus) at His right hand. Before He got there, He had an encounter with our hearts, infusing man with the distinctive aroma of His essence and glory. When someone accepts Christ, the Teabag—Jesus—is placed in his heart, and the radical tea transformation takes place; man is no longer just a man, but a man united to Christ.

The Teabag went into the "trash" (the grave), but was raised from the dead by the power of God and is now seated in heavenly places. Now, God looks at the cups—the vessels in His church—and says, "Ah, tea!" So, praise be to God, saints. We be tea! We're so united to Christ that we're literally His physical body in the earth. Jesus is the head of that body. You cannot separate the head from the body and have life. The good news is, we're no longer separated from Him; we're one spirit for eternity.

Now, just for the challenged among us (I'm not putting people down, but I've found over the years that some folks try hard to miss the point.), let's be clear here. I am not saying, "I'm God." I'm too dumb to be God, and you're too smart to think I'm God. I only qualify this because there's inevitably one person in the crowd who will say, "That's it, Gertrude! We're out of here!" And the wife will answer, "You're right, Elmer! We need to leave right now! He said he's God!" Oh brother! You might get mad at me for that, but I'd rather you get mad at me for being clear that you and I are not God than have you be mad at me because you think I said you and I are God. I repeat: You and I aren't God, but if you are truly a born-again believer, God is in you and you are in Him. I constantly thank God for this truth.

God is in us, working in and through us to change this sin-ridden world. By His Spirit, He dwells in us. We are not God, and He is not us. Yet together, we be tea. When the Father sees you and I, He sees Jesus in us and calls us the body of Christ—tea!

Some things Paul said take more than a casual glance to understand, but I assure you that all of us can by the Spirit receive understanding no matter how difficult it seems. I say this because some people believe there are things in the Word of God that are just too hard to comprehend, and they use the Word in a wrong way to back up their deception. For example, Peter mentioned how difficult some of Paul's writings were, but I want to emphasize that his comments were in a specific context and concerned a very particular group of people in the church.

> *And remember, our Lord's patience gives people time to be saved. This is what our beloved brother Paul also wrote to you with the wisdom God gave him—speaking of these things in all of his letters. Some of his comments are **hard to understand,** and those who are **ignorant** and **unstable** have twisted his letters to mean something quite different, just as they do with other parts of Scripture. And this will result in their destruction.*
>
> 2 Peter 3:15-16 NLT [Emphasis mine]

We're not to be ignorant and unstable, nor are we to have a heart that permits us to twist Scripture away from its true meaning. This would only create our own demise. God has given us His Spirit to reveal these mysteries to us for our edification.

> *But the natural man does not receive the things of the Spirit of God, for they are foolishness to him; nor can he know them, because they are spiritually discerned.*
>
> 1 Corinthians 2:14

The new creation realities are not discerned by natural men; they're spiritually discerned by spiritual men through the action of the Holy Spirit and the quickening power of God's Word.

God has made these mysteries easy for believers to understand when we're connected to the vine and seeing with spiritual eyes. Yes, they're hidden mysteries, but that's because there's an enemy devoid of love. These mysteries are concealed to keep him from knowing God's battle plan. They're also stowed away for the believer who senses their existence, like an invisible treasure that can be discovered and made manifestly real. God has done this for the believer to incite an unending desire to pursue and seek after the treasure, digging for the deep things of God. God's plan from the foundation of the world has been for His people to understand He is with us, He is among us, He is in us, and He is for us. His mysterious, marvelous, miraculous accomplishment through Christ—His making of tea—is as simple and yet profound as the air we breathe.

> *For to me, to live is Christ, and to die is gain.*
>
> Philippians 1:21

Wow! What a bombshell. Paul is not saying he is Christ. He is saying he is so united to Christ that his way of life was a living explanation of this new life we have in Christ.

> *I have been crucified with Christ; it is no longer I who live, but Christ lives in me; and the life which I now live in the flesh I live by faith in the Son of God, who loved me and gave Himself for me.*
>
> Galatians 2:20 [Emphasis mine]

I am not Jesus and Jesus is not me, but we be TEA!

Having revelation of God in you will change the sum total of your worldview. This revelation redesigns how you live, elevates your expectations, and propels you to victory. It gives you an awareness of

God's presence with you as you face all the obstacles and challenges of this life.

THE WAY JESUS SEES IT

> *But when the Son of Man comes in his glory, and all the angels with him, then he will sit upon his glorious throne. All the nations will be gathered in his presence, and he will separate the people as a shepherd separates the sheep from the goats. He will place the sheep at his right hand and the goats at his left. Then the King will say to those on his right, "Come, you who are blessed by my Father, inherit the Kingdom prepared for you from the creation of the world. For I was hungry, and you **fed me.** I was thirsty, and you gave **me a drink.** I was a stranger, and you **invited me into your home.** I was naked, and **you gave me clothing.** I was sick, and you cared for me. I was in prison, and **you visited me."***
>
> *Then these righteous ones will reply, "Lord, when did we ever see you hungry and feed you? Or thirsty and give you something to drink?" ...And the King will say, "I tell you the truth, **when you did it to one of the least of these my brothers and sisters, you were doing it to me!"***
>
> Matthew 25:31-37;40 NLT [Emphasis mine]

Jesus tells His sheep that whatever they have physically done to and for His people in the earth, they've literally done to and for Him personally. Jesus is emphatic that the people who make up His body here and now are one with Him in every way, and whatever is rendered for them is rendered for Him. Likewise, Jesus speaks to the goats, saying that whatever they've neglected to do for the body of Christ in the earth, they've neglected to do for Him. This is not just a theory or mere theology. We're united to Jesus in reality, completely and perfectly identified as in Him. This is the message of Grace—the unmerited favor of God that infuses us with His life and connects us with everything that is in heaven.

This was highlighted by the story of Paul's conversion on the road to Damascus. After the resurrection of Jesus, and because of great persecution against the church, Christianity began to spread throughout Jerusalem, in all Judaea, in Samaria, and unto the uttermost parts of the earth. Saul of Tarsus was the Pharisee leading the assault against Christians, bearing letters from the high priest and breathing out threats and slaughter against the disciples of the Lord.

When Jesus knocked Saul off his donkey to have a chat with him about his attitude toward the church, He said, "Saul, Saul, why are you persecuting **Me**?"

Undoubtedly shocked by the supernatural light shining round him, Saul asked, "Who are you, Lord?"

And the Lord responded, "I am Jesus, the One you are persecuting" (Acts 9:5 NLT).

Interestingly enough, Paul and Jesus had never seen each other in the flesh while Jesus was alive on the earth. When Jesus was walking daily with His disciples in Jerusalem and in the temple, Saul was away at "Bible school," sitting at the feet of Gamaliel being taught according to the perfect manner of the law of the fathers. Despite this proper background, Jesus made it clear to Saul that when he was persecuting the believers unto death, binding and delivering men and women into prison, he was actually doing it to Him. Jesus took it personally when Saul held the coats of those who stoned Stephen, consenting unto his death.

I know the church as a whole does not yet have a good understanding of this gift of love and power since it's obvious that we often don't treat each other very well. If God's people had the true revelation of Christ within, we would treat each other as if we were dealing with Jesus Himself. It's time we as a church take the commandment of the Lord seriously and daily set ourselves to grow in the discerning of His body.

> *A new commandment I give to you, that you love one another; as I have loved you, that you also love one another. By this all will know that you are My disciples, if you have love for one another.*
>
> John 13:34-35

The new commandment is superior to the old, which said: "You shall love the Lord your God with all your heart, with all your soul, with all your mind, and with all your strength...[and] love your neighbor as yourself" (Mark 12:30-31). Many people today don't love themselves with a healthy love, which establishes a poor benchmark for how they should treat others. The new commandment makes it clear that the standard for loving others is now the one Jesus has established in His Word, making us all without excuse. We are to love one another as Jesus loves us.

I personally set myself in prayer regularly: "God, continue to show me who I am. Show me my connection with you, because if I am miraculously united to you then so is my wife, so are my friends, so are all the people in this great church." Once we make a deliberate effort to grow in this understanding, it will become easier and easier to treat one another like Jesus.

Look at it this way. If I want to find my friend Richard—the person, Richard—I don't get really weird and hyper-spiritual. I don't sit in a corner with my legs crossed, my hands lifted, palms up, eyes closed, and start meditating and humming, "Ohmmm... I need to see

Richard. Ohmmm...." No, I actively start looking for his body. When I find his body, I expect him to be in it, and then I talk to him—while he is in his body. If I'm looking for Pastor Ann, I go looking for her, fully expecting her to be in her body. When I find her, I talk to Ann—the person, not her body. Her body isn't really what I'm looking for; I'm looking for Ann, and I expect her to be there in her body. The whole world is looking for God, and they're supposed to find Him in His body. They're supposed to come and take a sip of believers' lives and say "TEA!"

We, on the other hand, should say in humility, "I'm really just a vessel of water. When I called upon the name of the Lord, God put a Teabag in me, and that Teabag had such a profound impact on my inner man that now all you can taste is tea. And that same Teabag who sits at the right hand of the Father is patiently waiting to have the same life-changing impact on others." We have simply tasted and seen that the Lord is good. Jesus lives in His body—the body of Christ—and we as believers are all fitly joined together in that body so that the world can see Jesus. Then they, too, will be TEA.

When you are born again, you become the person God ordained you to be from the foundations of the world, and it's now up to you to recognize it and begin to live it. Look at this actuality through the paraphrase of Galatians 2:20 by Ben Campbell Johnson.

> *My pseudo-self which tried to get a relation with God by keeping the rules has been nailed to Christ's cross. My authentic self has come alive, yet I am not in isolation. I am united with Christ and I keep trusting in his love for me, especially as it went into action for me on the cross.*

Pseudo means: *Not actually being something, but having the appearance of it—resembling or imitating something.* In this world, we have pseudo-wrestlers (yes, I hate to break it to you, but it really is fake!). We have pseudo-journalists (I'm sorry, but I have to say it. The national media journalists are just political hacks for a liberal, progressive, backward agenda. They are merely disguised as actual journalists.) We have pseudo-preachers, and we have a ton of pseudo-Christians. The pseudo-Christians have the appearance of being Christians, but they have not been born again. They have not been united to Christ.

Their Christianity is a sham because they're merely doing religion, and their hearts are still darkened by the god of this world. These are the true hypocrites, the people who portray something on the outside while having no desire from the heart to be what they claim to be in the flesh. Before I really embraced Christ and let Him come into my life, I was a pretender. I acted a certain way around one group and a different way around another. I tried to be one way to please my parents and another way in the midst of friends, trying to be "cool" so I'd be accepted. I tried all sorts of "self-imposed identities" until I wore myself out and finally surrendered everything to Jesus.

In that day, my pseudo-self, my fallen, pathetic, lost self, was crucified with Christ. My authentic, God-ordained-self came alive, and the new me is united to Christ who loved me and gave Himself for me. I seek every day for His life to be established and apparent in me. I can now reach for the prize of the high calling of being who God appointed me to be. No more pretending! I'm not perfect after the flesh, but I no longer have to put on a fake public face to be accepted. I am completely accepted in the beloved according to the Word of God. "The beloved" in Scripture is a direct reference to Jesus. And not only am I accepted, but I am defended, for the Scripture also says, "If God is for us, who can be against us?"

(Romans 8:31 NLT). I am free to be me in Jesus. I'm comfortable with who God made me. I no longer have to hate myself, and I don't have to spend the rest of my life trying to be somebody I'm not.

So, let go of any pseudo-life. I pray you will embrace the new creation. It's a fresh you, a state-of-the-art you, an original, in-mint-condition you. If you will yield to God, you'll discover the wonder of it and say, "Oh! This is what God had in mind for me. I'm still a self, but I'm not a pseudo-self. My new self is united to Christ, and yeah, I may have a long way to go. I may be a work in progress, but what a difference Christ has made in me."

Because of grace—the empowering presence of God and the cross—we've been given a high Christ-esteem and a positive Christ-image. With a new identity, we have infinite value. The image we bear is not imposed by others, but rather by Christ Himself. When we wake up to the infusion of our spirit with Christ, we have what it takes to deny self (the old man in Adam), take up our cross (the power of God that brought an end to that pseudo-life), and follow Jesus. We be TEA.

But he who is joined to the Lord is one spirit with Him.

1 Corinthians 6:17

For we are members of His body, of His flesh and of His bones.

Ephesians 5:30

CHAPTER FIFTEEN
DESTINY & PURPOSE

Beholding your new identity in Christ affects your destiny. How we see ourselves affects everything we do and subsequently the fruit we bear. This is why it's so important to study the Word. It's the source of knowledge about ourselves, and it reveals our destiny. It takes time to search it out.

> *Whom shall he teach knowledge? and whom shall he make to understand doctrine? them that are weaned from the milk, and drawn from the breasts. For precept must be upon precept, precept upon precept; line upon line, line upon line; here a little, and there a little.*

Isaiah 28:9-10 KJV

Mary and Joseph were devout Jews who raised their children in the nurture and admonition of the Lord. Beginning when Jesus was a small child, they taught him precept upon precept and line upon line. Jesus learned who He was through the Word of God that bore witness with His Spirit that He was the Christ. And that is also exactly how we discover who we are.

5/5/21
Acts 23

Carolyn gone 5/17 - 5/26
(5/12 & 5/19)

*And when He was twelve years old, they went up to Jerusalem according to the custom of the feast. When they had finished the days, as they returned, the Boy Jesus lingered behind in Jerusalem. And Joseph and His mother did not know it; but supposing Him to have been in the company, they went a day's journey, and sought Him among their relatives and acquaintances. So when they did not find Him, they returned to Jerusalem, seeking Him. Now so it was that after three days they found Him in the temple, sitting in the midst of the teachers, both listening to them and asking them questions. And all who heard Him were astonished at His understanding and answers. So when they saw Him, they were amazed; and His mother said to Him, "Son, why have You done this to us? Look, Your father and I have sought You anxiously." And He said to them, "Why did you seek Me? Did you not know that I must be about **My Father's business?"***

Luke 2:42-49 [Emphasis mine]

At the age of twelve, Jesus discovered who He was and what He was sent to do. Mary and Joseph didn't reveal this mystery to Him. They simply led Him to the Word of God where His spirit bore witness with the truth. It was God the Father, and God alone, who revealed Jesus' identity. No man on earth could reveal it. The apostle Peter also saw this truth about Jesus by the power of the Holy Spirit. Every day he meditated in the Scriptures, and when Jesus confronted him, saying, "Who do men say that I am?" and "Whom do you say that I am?" he declared, "Thou art the Christ, the Son of the living God." Jesus answered, "Flesh and blood hath not revealed it unto thee, but my Father which is in heaven" (Matthew 16:13-17 KJV).

This signifies that the revelation of who you are in Christ can only come from the Father through the Word of God. Jesus, the pattern Son, perfectly demonstrated the path that all men are to take to receive this divine revelation from the Father. Jesus discovered Himself in the Scriptures. He saw that He came from the Father, He saw that His purpose was to destroy the works of Satan, and He saw the path He must take: the cross. More than all of that, He saw what joy was set before Him—being seated on the throne at the right hand of God and bringing many men to glory. His entire purpose and destiny were revealed through the Scriptures.

Our parents, friends, and college professors cannot really tell us who we are, where we came from, why we are here, or what our purpose is in life. God and only God has the answer to these questions and they are found in His Word, both written (Scriptures) and living (Jesus). Through a searching of the Scriptures and a personal relationship with the Lord, these mysteries are revealed to each of us.

> *Therefore, when He came into the world, He said: "Sacrifice and offering You did not desire, But a body You have prepared for Me. In burnt offerings and sacrifices for sin You had no pleasure. Then I said, 'Behold, I have come—**In the volume of the book it is written of Me**—To do Your will, O God.'" Previously saying, "Sacrifice and offering, burnt offerings, and offerings for sin You did not desire, nor had pleasure in them" (which are offered according to the law), then He said, "Behold, I have come to **do Your will, O God.**" He takes away the first that He may establish the second.*
>
> Hebrews 10:5-9 [Emphasis mine]

> *Search the scriptures; for in them ye think ye have eternal life: and they are **they which testify of me**. And ye will not come to me, that ye might have life.*
>
> John 5:39-40 KJV [Emphasis mine]

As a young boy growing up, Jesus searched the Scriptures daily, and the Father spoke to Him: "That's You, Lamb of God." "That's You, Immanuel." "That's You, Wonderful, Counselor, Mighty God, the Everlasting Father, the Prince of Peace." "That's You, seed of Abraham...Messiah...Son of David." Jesus discovered Himself and the scope of His destiny by looking into the volume of the Scriptures. We're to discover who we are and what we need to do in the volume of the same book with our spirit bearing witness in the Holy Ghost.

Even after the crucifixion, Jesus personally modeled the divine path to understanding the mystery of Christ in you, the hope of glory. There were two disciples walking on the road to Emmaus, both of whom were down-in-the-mouth about Jesus' death because they did not yet understand what had taken place at the cross. When Jesus showed up asking why they were so doom and gloom, these guys didn't even recognize Him. They said, "Where the heck have you been?! Haven't you heard what happened to Jesus in Jerusalem?!"

> *Then he said unto them, O fools, and slow of heart to believe all that the prophets have spoken: Ought not Christ to have suffered these things, and to enter into his glory? And beginning at Moses and all the prophets, he expounded unto them in all the scriptures the things **concerning himself.***
>
> Luke 24:25-27 KJV [Emphasis mine]

Jesus took these guys straight to the Word of God and said, "You see that right there. Look what Moses said:"

> *I will raise up for them a Prophet like you from among their brethren, and will put My words in His mouth, and He shall speak to them all that I command Him.*
>
> Deuteronomy 18:18

"That's me! You see that right there. Look what Isaiah said:'"

For unto us a child is born, unto us a son is given: and the government shall be upon his shoulder: and his name shall be called Wonderful, Counsellor, The mighty God, The everlasting Father, The Prince of Peace. Of the increase of his government and peace there shall be no end, upon the throne of David, and upon his kingdom, to order it, and to establish it with judgment and with justice from henceforth even for ever. The zeal of the LORD of hosts will perform this.

Isaiah 9:6-7 KJV

"That's me! You see that right there. Look what Malachi said:"

But for you who fear my name, the Sun of Righteousness will rise with healing in his wings. And you will go free, leaping with joy like calves let out to pasture.

Malachi 4:2 NLT

"That's me!"

The disciples listened to Jesus, and after being renewed in the spirit of their mind and made receptive to the Holy Scriptures, their eyes were opened. They knew Him. It is by our steadfast perseverance in the Scriptures and submission to the Spirit of God that we also will come to the revelation of Christ in us. It's vitally important for us to pursue this revelation of God's work on our behalf.

All purpose and destiny are wrapped up in the revelation of what Christ has done for us. God has put it on my heart to declare this truth over and over, with clarity and simplicity.

For this reason I will not be negligent to remind you always of these things, though you know and are established in the present truth. Yes, I think it is right, as long as I am

*in this tent, to stir you up by reminding you, knowing that
shortly I must put off my tent, just as our Lord Jesus Christ
showed me. Moreover I will be careful to ensure that you
always have a reminder of these things after my decease.*

2 Peter 1:12-15

I don't plan on dying anytime soon, but I do want to make sure
you're established in this present truth. I assure you that Satan
relentlessly will attack your identity throughout your life. You must
have these truths deeply embedded in the core of your being, so
you'll be able to stand against the wiles of the devil.

God uses the Scriptures to reveal the calculating patterns of the
devil against mankind, and nothing illustrates this more clearly than
Satan's attack on Jesus in the wilderness. In the book of Matthew,
we see Jesus being tempted by Satan in three distinct ways. Each
attack was directed at robbing Him of His identity. The first two
were a direct assault on who He was, and the third was a cunning
attempt to get Him to go horizontal for His value—looking to man
for His assurance. If the enemy can get us to go horizontal—to look
to things or others for our validation instead of remaining vertical in
relationship with the Father—then we're done for. This is the crux of
the matter. Mankind has been in an identity crisis. We must snap out
of our old, hazy pictures of ourselves and wake up to the marvelous
identity that we have in Jesus. We must choose what God's Word
says about us. This is exactly what Jesus did in the wilderness. He
refuted Satan and chose the Word.

*Then Jesus was led up by the Spirit into the wilderness to
be tempted by the devil. And when He had fasted forty days
and forty nights, afterward He was hungry. Now when the
tempter came to Him, he said, "**If You are the Son of God**,
command that these stones become bread." But He answered*

and said, "It is written, 'Man shall not live by bread alone, but by every word that proceeds from the mouth of God.'"

Matthew 4:1-4 [Emphasis mine]

When Satan tried to get Jesus to doubt who He was, Jesus simply turned to God's Word as the source of His identity. Jesus recognized that an attack on His identity was an assault on His destiny.

*Then the devil took Him up into the holy city, set Him on the pinnacle of the temple, and said to Him, "**If You are the Son of God**, throw Yourself down. For it is written: 'He shall give His angels charge over you,' and, 'In their hands they shall bear you up, Lest you dash your foot against a stone.' Jesus said to him, "It is written again, 'You shall not tempt the Lord your God.'"*

Matthew 4:5-7 [Emphasis mine]

Once again, Satan made a direct assault on Jesus' identity. He knew that if he could get Jesus to waiver in His identity, he could derail His destiny. He tried to get Jesus to prove who He was by some kind of action (doing vs. being). But Jesus knew who He was and had nothing to prove.

Again, the devil took Him up on an exceedingly high mountain, and showed Him all the kingdoms of the world and their glory. And he said to Him, "All these things I will give You if You will fall down and worship me." Then Jesus said to him, "Away with you, Satan! For it is written, 'You shall worship the Lord your God, and Him only you shall serve.'"

Matthew 4:8-10

In the first two temptations, Satan directly questioned Jesus: "If you're the Son of God... (then do this)." When that did not work, Satan tried to get Jesus to serve creation more than the Creator, offering Him unlimited wealth and power in the earth. Right from the start, as Jesus was entering His earthly ministry (the divine call on His life from the Father), Satan directly attacked His awareness of who God the Father called Him to be and how He was to accomplish the things God had laid out for Him to do. All three temptations were meant to confuse Him concerning His identity. If He did not have a firm grasp on who He was, He would be on shaky ground. Then the enemy would be able to derail His purpose in the earth.

Satan's tactics haven't changed a bit. If he can't get you to believe his lies and doubt who you are in Christ, he will try to draw you away with the cares of this world, the deceitfulness of riches, and the lusts of other things. He will try to get you to measure yourself by the world's standards—by what you have or don't have. I've seen so many good people who truly love God fall prey to this temptation, only to find themselves depressed, discouraged, empty, and unfulfilled. The Scriptures are clear that if your desire turns to riches instead of the Father of riches, you will err from the faith and pierce yourself through with many sorrows.

Nothing in this natural life brings happiness and contentment outside of a personal relationship with the Lord. The only true source of identity and sense of value is a loving relationship with the Creator, and He is the giver of material blessings that cannot be stolen. When our blessings come from Him, we are not in bondage to them. Our worldly possessions don't possess us, and we don't have to strive to keep them. He desires that we trust Him for all things and that we take our proper place within all of His creation—which is a position of godly power and authority, bringing peace and the word of reconciliation to others. As a Christian, you must make a clear decision to find your destiny and purpose as it is revealed in the Word—your new identity in Christ. All you are called to do is fulfilled when you go vertical to God as your exclusive source for everything in this life.

> *"Therefore do not worry, saying, "What shall we eat?"*
> *or "What shall we drink?" or "What shall we wear?" For*
> *after all these things the Gentiles seek. For your heavenly*
> *Father knows that you need all these things. But seek first the*
> *kingdom of God and His righteousness, and all these things*
> *shall be added to you.*

Matthew 6:31-33

Jesus Christ never changed His strategy. He consistently demonstrated how to overcome the snare of the enemy. Every time He was assaulted, He simply responded with the Word of God: "For it is written… It is written... It is written." This is how we overcome all trouble. We must be deeply rooted and grounded in the Word of God, always being prepared to give an answer to anyone—including the devil—of the hope that's in us.

> *And they overcame him by the blood of the Lamb and by*
> *the word of their testimony, and they did not love their lives to*
> *the death.*

Revelation 12:11

At the end of Jesus' ministry (and the end of His physical life on earth) Satan was still attacking His identity by bringing the same accusation against Him at the cross:

> *And saying, "You who destroy the temple and build it in*
> *three days, save Yourself!* ***If You are the Son of God****, come*
> *down from the cross."*

Matthew 27:40 [Emphasis mine]

This is profound. Satan's attack on Jesus' identity at the advent of His ministry was identical to the attack on Him at the end of it: "**If you are the Son of God....**"

> *Likewise the chief priests also, mocking with the scribes and elders, said, "He saved others; Himself He cannot save. If He is the King of Israel, let Him now come down from the cross, and we will believe Him. He trusted in God; let Him deliver Him now if He will have Him; for He said, '**I am the Son of God.**'"*
>
> Matthew 27:41-43 [Emphasis mine]

> *Even the two criminals crucified next to him joined in the mockery!*
>
> Matthew 27:44 MSG

> *And one of the malefactors which were hanged railed on him, saying,* **If thou be Christ, save thyself and us.**
>
> Luke 23:39 KJV [Emphasis mine]

Satan brought a direct assault on Jesus' identity first through the people who passed by, then through the priests with the scribes and elders, and eventually through one of the thieves. Satan tried to get Jesus to doubt who He was and to back out on the call on His life to save mankind. Satan literally worked on Him until Jesus said, "It is finished" and drew His last breath. And because Satan knows that your understanding of your identification with Christ is the key to you fulfilling your destiny, he will relentlessly attempt to derail you through the same deceptions...until you, too, draw your last breath in this earth. Satan's practice and trusted method of identity theft proved fruitless against Jesus. He remained certain, assured, and steadfast in His identity, securing His destiny and purpose.

The truth is, Jesus was on the cross because of who He is. He is the Son of God who was sent to redeem the sons of Adam from a life of sin and death, and He fulfilled that purpose to the glory of God. It's important you see that everything Jesus did came directly from His revelation of who He is and His acknowledgement that the devil would not let up the fight against Him. Satan will never back off from accusing you either. Unless you know who you are, what you have, and what you can do in Christ, you'll never fulfill God's will and plan for your life. You are a new creation, and as that new creation existing in union with Him, you're not only blessed, but you become a blessing to all you come in contact with. Satan does not want that to happen.

OUR PRIMARY PURPOSE

> *And we know that all things work together for good to them that love God, to them who are the called according to his purpose. For whom he did foreknow, he also did predestinate to* **be conformed to the image of his Son**, *that he might be the firstborn among many brethren. Moreover whom he did predestinate, them he also called: and whom he called, them he also justified: and whom he justified, them he also glorified.*

> Romans 8:28-30 KJV [Emphasis mine]

It's sad there has been so much misunderstanding of this scripture. Even worse are the abuses from many in church leadership who have kept people in bondage to lack and defeat all their lives. I digress a little here because without a clear understanding of what the sovereignty of God is, you also could fall prey to the same hardships. God isn't sitting in the heavenlies, throwing switches, and pushing buttons to make everything happen in the earth. He is absolutely in control, but He is not controlling everything.

Sovereignty literally means *self-governed*. From God's point of view, that means He has established the baseline of truth to which He holds Himself accountable. He has set laws in motion, and He has given man dominion in the earth. He has made the will of His heart known. God never does bad things to people in order to make something good come out of it. If He did, He would be in violation of His own Word that says:

> *Love does no harm to a neighbor; therefore love is the fulfillment of the law.*

> Romans 13:10

God is love, and for Him to hurt or harm someone to bring good out of it defies the very nature of who He is. Evil things happen to all of us in this life, but the Scriptures say our heavenly Father cannot precipitate that evil:

> *Let no one say when he is tempted, "I am tempted by God"; for God cannot be tempted by evil, nor does He Himself tempt anyone.*

> James 1:13

> *Do not be deceived, my beloved brethren. Every good gift and every perfect gift is from above, and comes down from the Father of lights, with whom there is no variation or shadow of turning.*

> James 1:16-17

> *The thief does not come except to steal, and to kill, and to destroy. I have come that they may have life, and that they may have it more abundantly.*

> John 10:10

Bad things happen to good people all the time, and if God was truly responsible for it, that would mean He is doing bad things to Himself continually (since you are His body). That doesn't even make "good Oklahoma sense!"

The truth of the matter is that God is continually taking all the bad, all the hurt, and all the pain that the devil (directly or indirectly through this fallen world) has afflicted you with, and He is working every single bit of it (even our stumblings and mistakes) for our good. He does this all because we love Him and are indeed called according to His purpose. Then, because God is really good that way, He tells you exactly what that purpose is: to be conformed to the image of His Son.

Every single human on this earth was created by God and predestined to be conformed to the image of Jesus. Some choose wisely, others not so much, but the negative part is not on God's end. Every individual person has the right to choose to fulfill (or not fulfill) the divine destiny that God has given.

> *The Lord is not slack concerning His promise, as some count slackness, but is longsuffering toward us, not willing that **any should perish** but that all should come to repentance.*
>
> 2 Peter 3:9 [Emphasis mine]

> *For this is good and acceptable in the sight of God our Saviour; Who will have all men to be saved, and to come unto the knowledge of the truth.*
>
> 1 Timothy 2:3-4 KJV

Don't ever let anyone convince you that God predestines certain people for heaven and others for hell! You can clearly see from the Scriptures that God foreknew you in your mother's womb, and He has always desired goodness for you. He has always been wooing you to Himself and sending messages about His Love for you. He has been crying out, "This is who you are in My Son Jesus! I made a way for you!" The predestination that the Scriptures refer to is the destiny of being conformed and transformed into the image of Christ. Hell was not created for people, but rather Satan and his demons (Matthew 25:41).

Isaiah said that hell had enlarged its mouth to receive the wicked (Isaiah 5:14). The explanation for this is that hell had to enlarge its mouth because God didn't will for anyone to go there. He created it just large enough for Satan and all renegade spirits. God does not send anyone to hell. Rather, people choose to go there by rejecting God's gift of eternal life. While God will honor your choice to go, He has made a way so no one has to go. That way is Jesus and the work of the cross and the resurrection from death.

Look again at Paul's statement in Romans 8:28. God never said that all things are good or that all things were of God. What He did say was:

> *...**All things work together for good to them that love** **God** [not everyone loves God], **to them who are called** **according to His purpose** [not our own purpose, whether in ignorance or in rebellion to God].*
>
> Romans 8:28 KJV [Emphasis and brackets mine]

Then, Paul ties God's purpose into the true meaning of predestination (being conformed to the image of His Son). God's plan and purpose is not based on the things that happen to us. It's based on the fact that if we love God, then we are "called according to His purpose." With this standard of truth, we can all know that God will work all of the bad things that happen in this life together for our good. This is spiritual formation (Christlikeness). Paul never intended to make predestination a matter of heaven or hell, and unfortunately, many people have come to a narrow belief that that's all there is. We will either be burning in a devil's hell for eternity or singing forever around the throne in heaven. I personally hope that's not all there is to eternity because standing around and singing forever isn't really comforting to me.

What I do know for certain is that God is a God of destiny and purpose, and a God of work and righteous judgment. He's a God who will forever be creating and expanding the new heaven and new earth that we'll be residing in long after this world has come to an end. This life is simply the training and proving ground for the next step in life with Him.

Simply put, predestination on God's part is that all be saved, and through salvation, we'll be conformed into the image of His dear Son. We know this because God is a good God and wants only good for everyone.

> *I call heaven and earth as witnesses today against you, that I have set before you life and death, blessing and cursing; therefore choose life, that both you and your descendants may live.*
>
> Deuteronomy 30:19

God doesn't will harm or bad for anyone, but He has given us all a choice. Because of poor lifestyle choices, people personally suffer and create suffering for others. This is the scriptural principle of sowing and reaping. Even though God wants only good for us, He does not necessarily wipe away the consequences of our poor decisions or the poor decisions of others. Ultimately, God's primary purpose for us is that we be Christlike (no hyphen) and that we make decisions rooted in our new identity and in His Word. That journey begins with your identification with Christ. As the Holy Spirit reveals to you who you really are, and guides you toward better lifestyle choices, He will transform your life.

> ...*that the sharing of your faith may become effective by the acknowledgment of every good thing which is in you in Christ Jesus.*
>
> Philemon 1:6

How can you acknowledge the good in you in Christ if you don't know it? How can your faith be effectual or working for you if you don't know the good that's in you in Christ? As you read the New Testament and see all the declarations of who you are, listen for Jesus to say, "That's you!" In discovering your new identity, you will fulfill your primary purpose—being conformed to the image of God's Son. You will overflow into what I refer to as your secondary purpose— filling the position and station God has called you to fulfill in this life.

That purpose may be fluid, changing from one step to another as you go through different seasons of maturing in life. But your spiritual transformation into the image of Christ is always the primary goal. What you do for a vocation is secondary (coach, teacher, truck driver, mom, singer, you name it!).

Discovering and fulfilling your purpose is vital to leading a fruitful life full of happiness and joy. When you know that you're on the pathway of God's purpose, all of life is good. Contrary to that, when you're not on that path, nothing in life seems to be good. What I want you to see in all this is that developing and walking in the purpose of God is really more about the journey than about the destination. We will all eventually come to the unity of the faith.

For now, we are all most definitely a work in progress, but we can still enjoy the discovery of our future and the recovery of our new identity in Jesus.

> *And He Himself gave some to be apostles, some prophets, some evangelists, and some pastors and teachers, for the equipping of the saints for the work of ministry, for the edifying of the body of Christ, till we all come to the unity of the faith and of the knowledge of the Son of God, to a perfect man, **to the measure of the stature of the fullness of Christ.***
>
> Ephesians 4:11-13 [Emphasis mine]

You must keep in mind that in our current earthly state, we see through a glass darkly. None of us have "arrived." The key to a successful life in Christ is not in the arriving, but in first just leaving—leaving the old life, the old man, the old identity. Untie your ship from the dock and start heading toward that destination where you will know the fullness of God's desire for you.

At Jesus' return, we will know Him face to face and come to that perfect revelation of Him. In the meantime, we simply need to continually press toward the mark of the prize of the high calling of God in Christ Jesus.

All believers have the same primary purpose: to be conformed to the image of Christ and fill the earth with His glory. All believers also have a secondary purpose, which is to fulfill the specific call of God on your life. My secondary purpose is to oversee and pastor Victory Life Church, sharing Jesus with a hurting generation. I was born and designed by God to do what I do—pastor and teach. How I perceive and work out my primary purpose (being conformed to Christ's image) directly affects the fruit of my secondary purpose (pastor/teacher). Whether you're a teacher, coach, accountant, evangelist, prophet, mechanic, business owner, or circus performer, if you miss your primary purpose, your secondary purpose will never evolve into all God ordained it to be.

Being conformed into Christ's image is the key to your secondary purpose. And that all begins with a revelation of who you are as a born-again believer, as God's kid, as a whole new creation, as more than a conqueror. Determine to receive this revelation and then go forth and conquer!

A DIFFERENT ATTITUDE

> *These things I have spoken to you, [God's word] that in Me [new identification] you may have peace. In the world you will have tribulation;* **but be of good cheer,** *I have overcome the world.*
>
> John 16:33 [Emphasis and brackets mine]

You can be happy and of "good cheer." In Christ, your identity is that of an overcomer. I am so passionate about this—I want to shout this at you! I shout it at myself! *I am an overcomer, not overcome. I am more than a conqueror through Him that loved me.* Everything within me screams, "I am a victor, not a victim!" I will rejoice, and I will go through life with the attitude of a winner.

We all should have this good attitude. We all should have positive expectations because right here and right now, in everyday life, we are victorious in Christ.

Your new identity in Christ trumps your old identity in Adam hands down! The identity theft perpetrated on Adam in the garden and passed down to us all has been gloriously reversed in Jesus. My new identity in Christ is awesome and the source of all the good in my life. Thank you, Jesus!

ABOUT THE AUTHOR

Duane Sheriff leads Victory Life Church, a growing multi-campus church based in Durant, Oklahoma, where he has been the senior pastor for more than thirty years. After having a life-changing encounter with Jesus in 1980, Duane left a promising tennis career, married his wife, Sue, and moved from Florida to Oklahoma to attend Bible school. He has been actively involved in ministry ever since.

Under his leadership, Victory Life Church has grown from meeting in a small double-wide trailer to thousands of people each weekend meeting in multiple campuses across the United States and online across the globe. His passion is to build healthy churches that are growing people in Christ, helping people discover their true identities and become all God created them to be.

Duane is a highly sought-after international speaker and has given away millions of free teachings through his ministry. Duane and Sue have four adult children who are all active in ministry. When he's not pastoring or teaching, Duane enjoys hunting and spending time with his family, especially the grandkids.

For more information or teachings go to pastorduane.com or contact us at dsm@pastorduane.com. Be sure to subscribe to our YouTube channel. You can find us at Duane Sheriff Ministries.

SPECIAL NOTE FROM THE AUTHOR

The apostle Paul in Colossians 1:24-27 speaks of a mystery which has been hidden from ages and from generations, but now is made manifest and is Christ in us, the hope of glory.

> *I now rejoice in my sufferings for you, and fill up in my flesh what is lacking in the afflictions of Christ, for the sake of His body, which is the church, of which I became a minister according to the stewardship from God which was given to me for you, to fulfill the word of God, **the mystery** which has been hidden from ages and from generations, but now has been revealed to His saints. To them God willed to make known what are the riches of the glory of this mystery among the Gentiles: which is Christ in you, the hope of glory.*
>
> Colossians 1:24-27 [Emphasis mine]

This mystery is the restoration of your identity from being in Adam to being in Christ. I hope that through the pages of this book, you have begun to discover that mystery in your life. The understanding of this mystery is just the beginning, and now we can begin to walk out the impact of that mystery in our lives. It's a wonderful journey of exploring the relationship we have with Christ and transforming our lives to be more like Him. The mystery mentioned in Colossians is the start of this journey. The rest of the journey now becomes what Paul described in Ephesians 5:32 as a "great mystery."

> *This is a **great mystery**, but I speak concerning Christ and the church.*
>
> Ephesians 5:32 [Emphasis mine]

Paul speaks of this "great mystery" between Christ and the church, and between a husband and a wife as one flesh.

On the day of your wedding, you begin a new life. You are now bound as husband and wife together in love. But as we all know, a wedding doesn't make a marriage. As each year of marriage comes around, you deepen that relationship, discover new things about each other, and grow in your married identity. The wedding is like the mystery mentioned in Colossians, but the marriage is what Paul described in Ephesians as a great mystery.

In this book, we unpacked the mystery of our new identity. We discovered the unveiling of that mystery and the relationship of love between us and Christ, the new creation. But it does not end there. Now, we're bound to understand the great mystery of our identity in Christ and what this new relationship will evolve into over time.

We're now ready for the Holy Spirit to continually reveal more to us as our relationship with Jesus Christ grows. This great mystery is a topic that I could not include in this book but will be sharing in my next book, an epic love story of marriage and our new identity in Jesus as our husband.

I pray that the recovery of your new identity in Jesus is as exciting as mine has been and that people see Jesus, the hope of glory, in you.

Blessings,

Duane Sheriff

PRAYER OF SALVATION

God loves you—no matter who you are, no matter what your past. God loves you so much that He gave His one and only begotten Son for you. The Bible tells us that "...whoever believes in him shall not perish but have eternal life" (John 3:16 NIV). Jesus laid down His life and rose again so that we could spend eternity with Him and experience His absolute best on earth. If you would like to receive Jesus into your life, say the following prayer out loud and mean it in your heart.

> *Heavenly Father, I come to you admitting that I am a sinner. Right now, I choose to turn away from sin, and I ask you to cleanse me of all unrighteousness. I believe that Your Son, Jesus, died on the cross to take away my sins. I also believe that He rose again from the dead so that I might be forgiven of my sins and made righteous through faith in Him. I call upon the name of Jesus Christ to be the Savior and Lord of my life. Jesus, I choose to follow You and ask that You fill me with the power of the Holy Spirit. I declare that right now I am a child of God. I am free from sin and full of the righteousness of God. I am saved in Jesus' name. Amen.*

If you prayed this prayer to receive Jesus Christ as your Savior for the first time, please write to us to receive a free book!

Harrison House Publishers
P.O. Box 310
Shippensburg, Pennsylvania 17257-0310
www.harrisonhouse.com

The Harrison House Vision

Proclaiming the truth and the power

of the Gospel of Jesus Christ with excellence.

Challenging Christians

to live victoriously,

grow spiritually,

know God intimately.

Connect with us on

f Facebook @ HarrisonHousePublishers

and ⃝ Instagram @ HarrisonHousePublishing

so you can stay up to date with news

about our books and our authors.

Visit us at **www.harrisonhouse.com**

for a complete product listing as well as

monthly specials for wholesale distribution.